Southeast Regional Assessment Project for the National Climate Change and Wildlife Science Center, U.S. Geological Survey

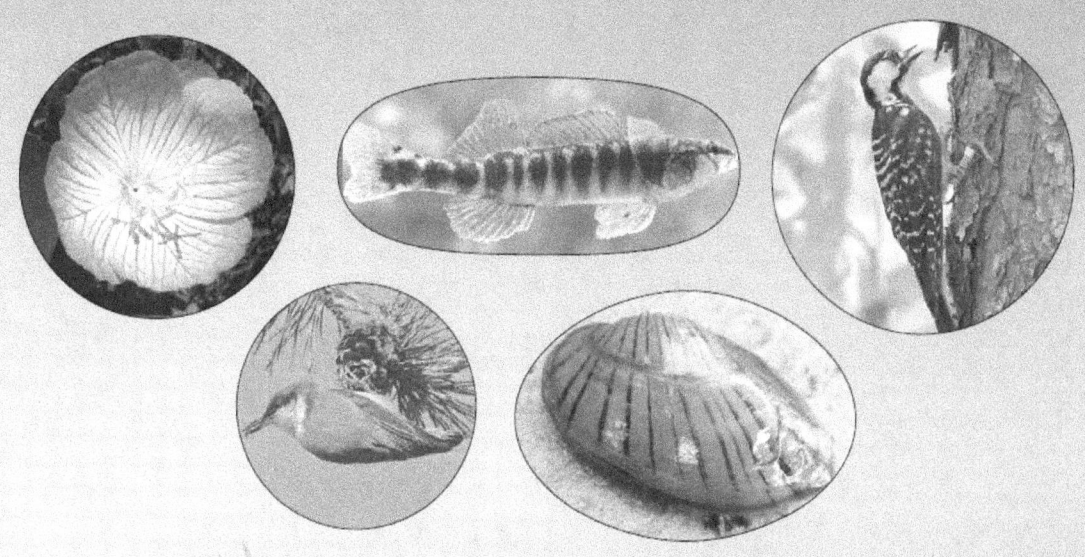

Open-File Report 2010–1213

U.S. Department of the Interior
U.S. Geological Survey

Southeast Regional Assessment Project for the National Climate Change and Wildlife Science Center, U.S. Geological Survey

Compiled by Melinda S. Dalton and Sonya A. Jones

Chapter I
Developing Regionally Downscaled Probabilistic Climate Change Projections
By Adam Terando, Murali Haran, and Katharine Hayhoe

Chapter II
Integrated Coastal Assessment
By Nathaniel Plant, Glenn R. Guntenspergen, K. Van Wilson, Scott Wilson, Cindy Thatcher, Alexa McKerrow, and Adam Terando

Chapter III
Integrated Terrestrial Assessment
By Alexa McKerrow, Adam Terando, Steve G. Williams, Jaime A. Collazo, James Grand, James D. Nichols, J. Andrew Royle, and John R. Sauer

Chapter IV
Multi-Resolution Assessment of Potential Climate Change Effects on Biological Resources: Aquatic and Hydrologic Dynamics
By James Peterson, Lauren Hay, Kenneth Odom, W. Brian Hughes, Robert Jacobson, John Jones, and Mary Freeman

Chapter V
Optimal Conservation Strategies to Cope With Climate Change
By James Grand

Chapter VI
Development and Dissemination of High-Resolution National Climate Change Dataset
Jaime Collazo, Lauren Hay, Katharine Hayhoe, Nathaniel Booth, and Adam Terando

Open-File Report 2010–1213

U.S. Department of the Interior
U.S. Geological Survey

U.S. Department of the Interior
KEN SALAZAR, Secretary

U.S. Geological Survey
Marcia K. McNutt, Director

U.S. Geological Survey, Reston, Virginia: 2010

For more information on the USGS—the Federal source for science about the Earth, its natural and living resources, natural hazards, and the environment, visit *http://www.usgs.gov* or call 1-888-ASK-USGS

For an overview of USGS information products, including maps, imagery, and publications,
visit *http://www.usgs.gov/pubprod*

To order this and other USGS information products, visit *http://store.usgs.gov*

Suggested citation:
Dalton, M.S., and Jones, S.A., comps., 2010, Southeast Regional Assessment Project for the National Climate Change and Wildlife Science Center, U.S. Geological Survey: U.S. Geological Survey Open-File Report 2010–1213, 38 p.

Contents

Executive Summary 1
Chapter I.   Developing Regionally Downscaled Probabilistic Climate Change Projections...........5
   Introduction...5
   Objectives...6
   Relations to Other Ongoing and Proposed Research 6
   Approach...6
      Global Climate Change Dataset..6
   Methods..7
      Earth Model of Intermediate Complexity 7
      Statistically Downscaled Simulation 8
      Bayesian Data-Model Fusion 8
      Projections of Impact-Relevant Climate Indicators 8
   References...9
Chapter II.   Integrated Coastal Assessment 11
   Introduction...11
   Objectives and Approach..12
      Objective 1—Land-Surface Elevation Changes 12
      Objective 2—Visualization 13
      Objective 3—Ecosystem Changes 15
   References...16
Chapter III.   Integrated Terrestrial Assessment 19
   Introduction...19
   Objectives and Approach..20
      Objective 1—Assessing Potential Impacts of Climate Change on Priority Habitats......20
      Objective 2—Assess Patch and Range Dynamics of Avian Species in
            Response to Land Use Patterns and Climate Change...22
   References...24
Chapter IV.   Multi-Resolution Assessment of Potential Climate Change Effects on
      Biological Resources: Aquatic and Hydrologic Dynamics...25
   Introduction...25
   Methods 26
      Phase I—Component Models 26
         Assessing Climate Change Effects on Biota 27
      Phase II—Model Refinement 28
   References...29
Chapter V.   Optimal Conservation Strategies to Cope With Climate Change 31
   Introduction...31
   Objectives..32
   Workshops 32
   References...34

Chapter VI.   Development and Dissemination of High-Resolution National
          Climate Change Dataset 35
     Introduction..35
          Background..35
     Methods..36
          Downscaled Climate Projections 36
          Geo Data Portal 36
          Workshops 38
     Summary...38
     References...38

Acronyms and Abbreviations Used in this Report

AAP	Adaptive Application Partnership
ACF	Apalachicola–Chattahoochee–Flint
AM	Adaptive Management
AOGCM	Atmosphere-Ocean Global Climate Model
AVHRR	Advanced Very High Resolution Radiometer
BBS	Breeding Bird Survey
BMA	Bayesian model averaging
CFWRU	Cooperative Fish and Wildlife Research Unit
CMIP	Climate Model Diagnosis and Intercomparison
CO_2	carbon dioxide
CRP	Conservation Reserve Program
DEM	digital elevation model
DOI	Department of the Interior
EMIC	Earth Model of Intermediate Complexity
ESCM	Earth System Climate Model
ETM+	enhanced thematic mapper plus scanner
ft	foot
FWS	U.S. Fish and Wildlife Service
GAP	Gap Analysis Program
GCM	Global Climate Model
GDP	Geo Data Portal
GHCN	Global Historic Climate Network
GHG	greenhouse gasses
GIS	Geographic Information System
HSI	habitat suitability indices

IFSAR	Interferometric Synthetic Aperture Radar
IPCC	Intergovernmental Panel on Climate Change
km	kilometer
LCC	Landscape Conservation Cooperative
LiDAR	Light Detection and Ranging
LULC	land use-land cover
m	meter
mm	millimeter
MSS	Multispectral Scanner
NALC	North American Landscape Characterization
NCCWSC	National Climate Change and Wildlife Science Center
NCDC	National Climatic Data Center
NCEP	National Center for Environmental Prediction
NCSU	North Carolina State University
NED	National Elevation Dataset
NGOM	Northern Gulf of Mexico
NLCD	National Land Cover Dataset
NOAA	National Oceanic and Atmospheric Administration
PDF	probability density function
ppm	parts per million
PRMS	Precipitation Runoff Modeling System
PSU	Pennsylvania State University
RCSC	Regional Climate Science Center
SAMBI	South Atlantic Migratory Bird Initiative
SERAP	Southeast Regional Assessment Project
SET	Surface Elevation Tables
SHC	Strategic Habitat Conservation
SLAMM	Sea Level Rise Affecting Marshes Model
SLEUTH	Slope, Land use, Exclusion, Transportation, and Hillshade
SNTEMP	Stream Network Temperature model
SRES	Special Report on Emission Scenarios
TELSA	Tool for Exploratory Landscape Scenario Analyses
TIGER	Topographically Integrated Geographic Encoding and Referencing
TM	Thematic Mapper
USGCRP	U.S. Global Change Research Program
USGS	U.S. Geological Survey
VDDT	Vegetation Dynamics Development Tool

Southeast Regional Assessment Project for the National Climate Change and Wildlife Science Center, U.S. Geological Survey

Compiled by Melinda S. Dalton and Sonya A. Jones

Executive Summary

The Southeastern United States spans a broad range of physiographic settings and maintains exceptionally high levels of faunal diversity. Unfortunately, many of these ecosystems are increasingly under threat due to rapid human development, and management agencies are increasingly aware of the potential effects that climate change will have on these ecosystems. Natural resource managers and conservation planners can be effective at preserving ecosystems in the face of these stressors only if they can adapt current conservation efforts to increase the overall resilience of the system. Climate change, in particular, challenges many of the basic assumptions used by conservation planners and managers. Previous conservation planning efforts identified and prioritized areas for conservation based on the current environmental conditions, such as habitat quality, and assumed that conditions in conservation lands would be largely controlled by management actions (including no action). Climate change, however, will likely alter important system drivers (temperature, precipitation, and sea-level rise) and make it difficult, if not impossible, to maintain recent historic conditions in conservation lands into the future. Climate change will also influence the future conservation potential of non-conservation lands, further complicating conservation planning. Therefore, there is a need to develop and adapt effective conservation strategies to cope with the effects of climate and landscape change on future environmental conditions.

Congress recognized this important issue and authorized the U.S. Geological Survey (USGS) National Climate Change and Wildlife Science Center (NCCWSC; http://nccw.usgs.gov/) in the Fiscal Year 2008. The NCCWSC will produce science that will help resource management agencies anticipate and adapt to climate change impacts to fish, wildlife, and their habitats. With the release of Secretarial Order 3289 on September 14, 2009, the mandate of the NCCWSC was expanded to address climate change-related impacts on all U.S. Department of the Interior (DOI) resources. The NCCWSC will establish a network of eight DOI Regional Climate Science Centers (RCSCs) that will work with a variety of partners to provide natural resource managers with tools and information that will help them anticipate and adapt conservation planning and design for projected climate change. The forecasting products produced by the RCSCs will aid fish, wildlife, and land managers in designing suitable adaptive management approaches for their programs.

The DOI also is developing Landscape Conservation Cooperatives (LCCs) as science and conservation action partnerships at subregional scales. The USGS is working with the Southeast Region of the U.S. Fish and Wildlife Service (FWS) to develop science collaboration between the future Southeast RCSC and future LCCs. The NCCWSC Southeast Regional Assessment Project (SERAP) will begin to develop regional downscaled climate models, land cover change models, regional ecological models, regional watershed models, and other science tools. Models and data produced by SERAP will be used in a collaborative process between the USGS, the FWS, (LCCs), State and federal partners, nongovernmental organizations, and academia to produce science at appropriate scales to answer resource management questions.

The SERAP will produce an assessment of climate change, and impacts on land cover, ecosystems, and priority species in the region (fig. 1). The predictive tools developed by the SERAP project team will allow end users to better understand potential impacts of climate change and sea level rise on terrestrial and aquatic populations in the Southeastern United States.

The SERAP capitalizes on the integration of five existing projects: (1) the Multi-State Conservation Grants Program project "Designing Sustainable Landscapes," (2) the USGS multidisciplinary Science Thrust project "Water Availability for Ecological Needs," (3) the USGS Southeast Pilot Project "Climate Change in the Southeastern U.S. and its Impacts on Bird Distributions and Habitats," (4) a sea-level rise impacts study envisioned jointly with the National Oceanic and Atmospheric Administration (NOAA), and (5) two USGS sea-level rise impact assessment projects that address inundation hazards and provide probabilistic forecasts of coastal geomorphic change. The SERAP will expand on these existing projects and include the following tasks, which were initiated in summer 2009:

- Regionally downscaled probabilistic climate-change projections

- Integrated coastal assessment

- Integrated terrestrial assessment

- Multi-resolution assessment of potential climate change effects on biological resources: aquatic and hydrologic dynamics

- Optimal conservation strategies to cope with climate change

The SERAP seeks to formally integrate these tasks to aid conservation planning and design so that ecosystem management decisions can be optimized for providing desirable outcomes across a range of species and environments.

The following chapters detail SERAP's efforts in providing a suite of regional climate, watershed, and landscape-change analyses and develop the interdisciplinary framework required for the biological planning phases of adaptive management and strategic conservation. The planning phase will include the identification of conservation alternatives, development of predictive models and decision support tools, and development of a template to address similar challenges and goals in other regions. The project teams will explore and develop ways to link the various ecological models arising from each component. The SERAP project team also will work closely with members of the LCCs (fig. 2) and other partnerships throughout the life of the project to ensure that the objectives of the project meet resources mangers needs in the Southeast.

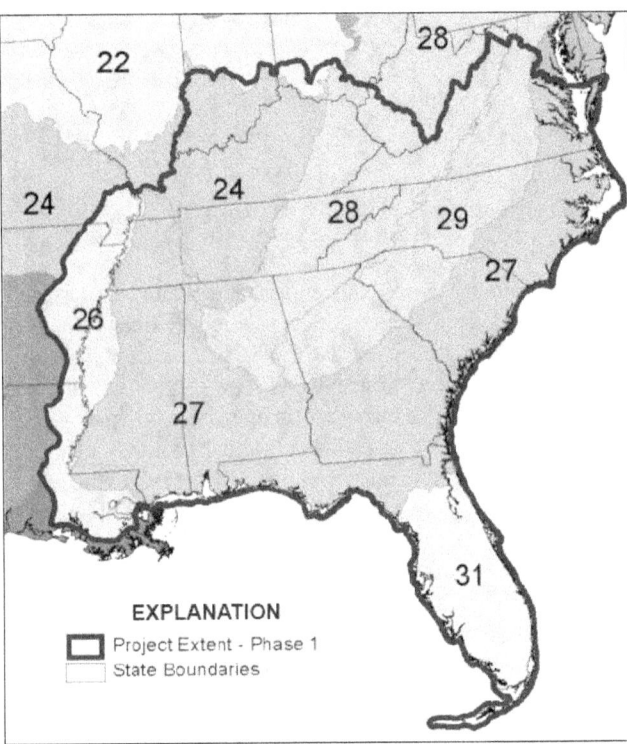

EXPLANATION

☐ Project Extent - Phase 1
☐ State Boundaries

North American Bird Conservation Initiative Bird Conservation Regions

24   Central Hardwoods Bird Conservation Region
26   Mississippi Alluvial valley Bird Conservation Region
27   Southeastern Coastal Plain Bird Conservation Region
28   Appalachian Mountains Bird Conservation Region
29   Piedmont Bird Conservation Region
31   Peninsular Florida Bird Conservation Region

Figure 1.   Study area for Southeast Regional Assessment Project.

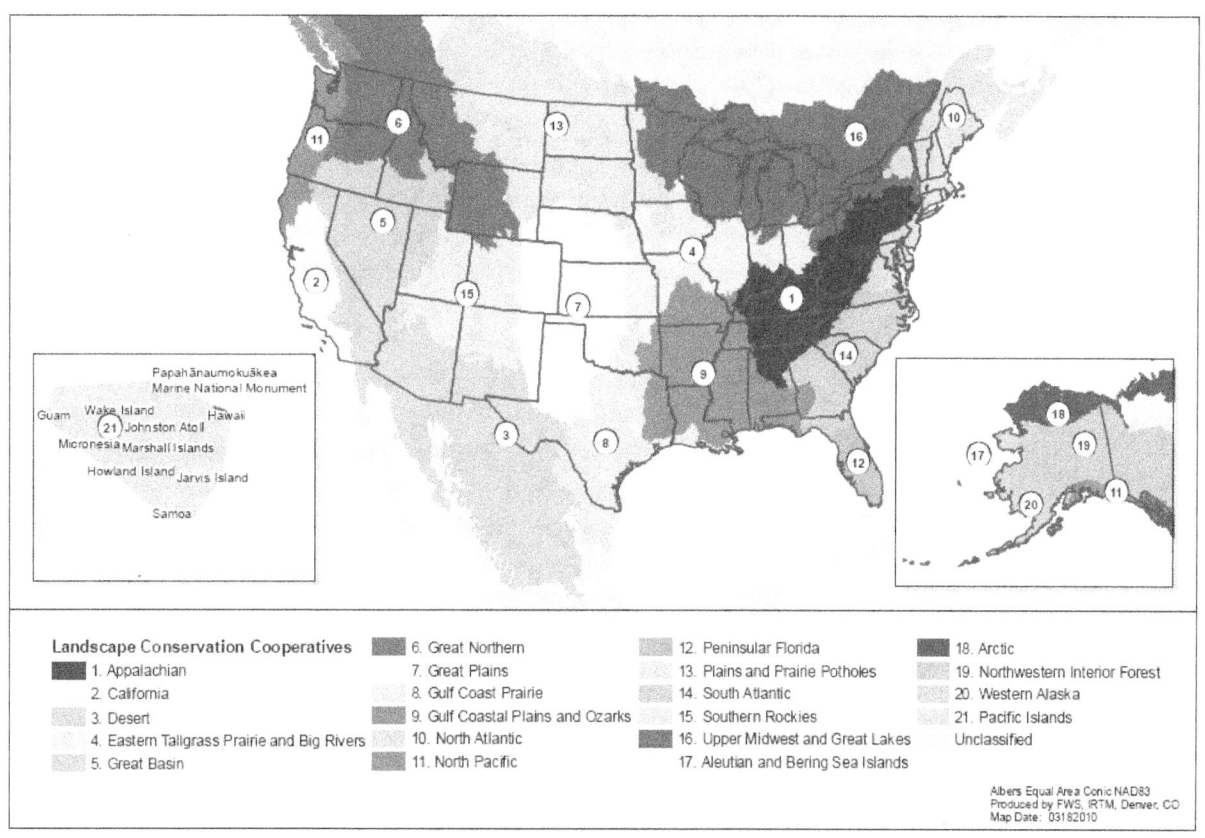

Figure 2. U.S. Fish and Wildlife Service Landscape Conservation Cooperatives (*http://www.fws.gov/science/shc/pdf/LCCMap.pdf*).

Chapter I.   Developing Regionally Downscaled Probabilistic Climate Change Projections

By Adam Terando, Murali Haran, and Katharine Hayhoe

Introduction

We propose to develop the core climatic datasets necessary to project regional ecosystem impacts resulting from 21st century climate change. We will adhere to an approach that carefully assesses and propagates model uncertainty, downscales climate projections to the scale of important ecosystem processes, and focuses on the most impact-relevant climatic variables. In doing so we will address three questions: (1) what is the magnitude and direction of climate change expected in the U.S. Southeast over the next 100 years, (2) how do the projected changes in climate relate to those parameters that most affect ecosystem processes specific to the Southeast, and (3) what is the level of uncertainty associated these projections?

Our approach improves upon many existing impact assessments by incorporating Global Climate Models (GCMs) from the Fourth Assessment Report of the Intergovernmental Panel on Climate Change (IPCC AR4), providing new information for decision makers through an improved quantifiable uncertainty analysis and providing seamless downscaled ecosystem-relevant climate products for the entire Southeast. We describe the input datasets we will use, our methodological approach, and the products to be used by collaborators in the Southeast Hub of the NCCWSC and the broader research community.

The Southeastern United States contains the highest levels of biodiversity in North America outside of the tropics (Jose and others, 2006). This is due in no small part to the climate the region has experienced over the last few millennia, characterized by abundant precipitation, mild temperatures, and low climatic variability. Recently, the IPCC AR4 concluded that it is very likely that humans are largely responsible for increasing the global average surface temperature by 1.0 degree Celsius in the 20th century through the release of greenhouse gasses (GHG) such as carbon dioxide (CO_2) into the atmosphere (Bernstein and others, 2008). This warming is expected to continue well into the future and is projected to cause sizable impacts on managed and unmanaged ecosystems (U.S. Climate Change Science Program, 2009). Thus, mitigation of, and adaptation to, the impacts of climate change on ecosystems in the Southeast will likely be the key challenge confronting natural resource managers in the coming decades.

Central to this is deciding how to best implement an adaptive management strategy given the large uncertainty associated with climate-change projections. Because of the coarse resolution of the models, addressing this issue requires a careful treatment of climate-change uncertainty as well as methods to downscale the model projections to the scale of ecosystem processes. The typical approach in impact assessments is to use one or more GCMs (known as a GCM ensemble) to project future climate change based on GHG emission scenarios. Often the uncertainty estimate for future climate change projections is given as the range of GCM output, which may expand as more models are added to the set. However, this method can underestimate the true structural and parametric uncertainty associated with the climate-change projections (fig. 1). This underestimation of uncertainty will then propagate through all levels of the regional assessment that require projections of climate change, leading to overconfident predictions. As a result, decision makers may insufficiently hedge against the risks associated with extreme climatic events that have a low probability of occurrence but the potential to be high-impact events. Thus a severe drought or a 500-year flood event, while having a low probability of occurrence in any given year, still must be incorporated into decision making because of its high environmental, social, and economic costs.

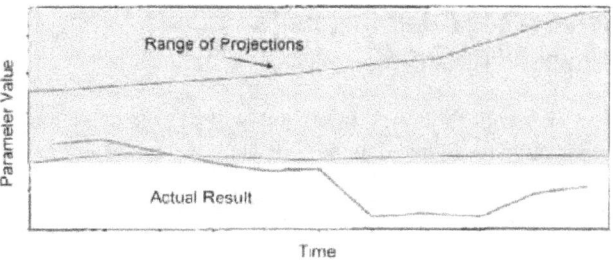

Figure 1.   Stylized example of underestimation of structural uncertainty leading to overconfident predictions as a result of assuming that the full range of uncertainty is equivalent to the number of models in the set (adapted from Draper, 1995).

Moreover, uncertainty also arises from the computational limits of GCMs. While global-scale climate changes are reasonably depicted by GCMs, many of the unique regional signals that result from large-scale interactions with distinctive geographic characteristics cannot be resolved. In addition, these limits also often result in truncated distributions of key variables such that high-impact climate extremes are ignored. Consequently, most GCMs still have resolutions that are too coarse compared to the scale at which many ecosystem impacts occur. High-resolution regional projections of climate change are required to accurately evaluate how climate change is likely to affect a given system. Statistical and dynamic downscaling approaches are often used to resolve these sub-grid scale processes, mitigate model biases, and correct for undersampling of the tails of distributions, thus helping to better characterize the uncertainty (see Hayhoe and others, 2008). These approaches are also subject to the same types of structural and parametric uncertainty that must be taken into account for a regional assessment in order for decision makers to understand the full range and likelihood of possible outcomes.

Objectives

- Design and run an ensemble of dozens of model runs using an Earth Model of Intermediate Complexity (EMIC) to characterize the effects of parametric uncertainty on climate projections in the United States;

- Downscale EMIC and IPCC projections of climate variables most relevant to range and habitat dynamics;

- Perform a Bayesian data-model fusion to weight the downscaled climate projections according to their performance and the structural uncertainty between models; and

- Integrate climate change projections into the full SERAP by disseminating the high resolution downscaled temperature and precipitation datasets and by developing derived climate products for the Southeast Science Hub collaborators.

Relations to Other Ongoing and Proposed Research

The products from this research will be used by all other research teams involved in the SERAP. It is important for resource managers and decision makers to have information about those particular climate variables in a region that will have the greatest impact on the dominant processes and disturbances that drive ecosystem function. For example, insect outbreaks are a common ecosystem disturbance, but the magnitude, extent, and frequency of an event is often limited by some temperature threshold related to biological activity and fitness, a threshold which may vary from species

to species and from region to region. Similarly, drought is a pervasive climatic disturbance but the effect of changing drought frequency and intensity will depend on the tolerance and vulnerability of the individual species of interest within the ecosystem. Working with the core team of ecologists, biologists, and hydrologists of the SERAP we have developed the following list of climate product deliverables (table 1).

Approach

The research methodology relies on state-of-the-art, well-documented models, data, and statistical tools. These include (1) Coupled Atmosphere-Ocean Global Climate Model (AOGCM) simulations from the IPCC AR) database archived by the Program for Climate Model Diagnosis and Intercomparison (CMIP); (2) an EMIC, the University of Victoria's Earth System Climate Model (ESCM; see Weaver and others, 2007; Schmittner and others, 2008); (3) statistically downscaled simulations forced by boundary conditions from 16 GCMs, the ESCM, and long-term daily weather records and re-analysis data at stations and grid-points archived by the National Climatic Data Center (NCDC) and the National Center for Environmental Prediction (NCEP); and (4) Bayesian ensemble dressing methods developed to address structural uncertainty and the accuracy of the AOGCMs. This section describes these tools, models, and datasets, and discusses their use in this project.

Global Climate Model Dataset

Global Climate Model (AOGCM) simulations. To include a representative range of forcing fields from AOGCMs, we propose to use historical and future simulations from one of each of the 16 different modeling groups that contributed to the IPCC AR4 database. Basic information about the models is provided online[1]. Historical 20C3M simulations will be used for 1900–1999. The 20C3M simulations represent each modeling group's best efforts to reproduce observed climate over the past century. As such, they include forcing from anthropogenic emissions of greenhouse gases, aerosols, and reactive species; changes in solar output; particulate emissions from volcanic eruptions; changes in tropospheric and stratospheric ozone; and other influences required to provide a comprehensive picture of climate over the last century. Using these historical simulations, the ability of selected models to simulate regional atmospheric dynamics and surface climate patterns over North America has been previously evaluated in Hayhoe and others (2007) and Vrac and others (2007). Some model biases and inter-model differences emerged, particularly at higher temporal (seasonal to monthly) and spatial scales, but in general the models were able to reproduce primary seasonal patterns and climate features.

---

[1] Model information available at *http //www-pcmdi.llnl.gov/ipcc/about.php.*

Table 1.   Direct and derived climate model products for use in the Southeast Regional Assessment project.

Climate Product	Source	Spatial Resolution	Temporal Resolution	Relationship to Integrated Assessment Components
Maximum Temperature	Direct Output	1/8"	Daily	Hydrologic Dynamics and Species Range Dynamics
Minimum Temperature	Direct Output	1/8"	Daily	Hydrologic Dynamics and Species Range Dynamics
Precipitation	Direct Output	1/8"	Daily	Hydrologic Dynamics and Species Range Dynamics
Evapotranspiration	Derived Product	1/8"	Daily	Hydrologic Dynamics and Species Range Dynamics
Solar Radiation	Derived Product	1/8"	Daily	Hydrologic Dynamics
Drought Index	Derived Product	1/8" - Eco-Region	Weekly	Hydrologic Dynamics, Aquatic Modeling, Species Range Dynamics, Vegetation Dynamics, Carbon Sequestration
Fire Frequency	Derived Product	Eco-Region	Monthly	Vegetation Dynamics, Carbon Sequestration
Frost Days	Derived Product	1/8"	Annual	Species Range Dynamics
Growing Season Length	Derived Product	1/8"	Annual	Species Range Dynamics
Insect Outbreak	Derived Product	Eco-Region	Annual	Species Range Dynamics, Carbon Sequestration

Future AOGCM simulations (2000–2099) will be based on the IPCC Special Report on Emission Scenarios (SRES, Nakićenović and others, 2000): higher (A1FI), mid-high (A2), mid (A1B), and lower (B1) emissions scenarios. These scenarios use projections of changes in population, demographics, technology, international trade, and other socio-economic factors to estimate corresponding emissions of greenhouse gases and other radiatively active atmospheric species. Although the SRES scenarios do not include any explicit policies aimed at reducing greenhouse gas emissions to mitigate climate change, the B1 scenario can be seen as proxy for stabilizing atmospheric CO_2 concentrations at or above 550 parts per million (ppm), as levels reach this value by 2100. Atmospheric CO_2 concentrations for the higher A1FI scenario are 970 ppm by 2100, and 830 ppm for A2. Input from these scenarios used to drive the future AOGCM simulations includes regional changes in emissions of greenhouse gases, particulates, and reactive species.

Earth Model of Intermediate Complexity. In order to improve the representation of parametric uncertainty, we will employ an EMIC (the ESCM) that enables production of many climate simulations (each for a different choice of model parameters). An EMIC is not a fully coupled AOGCM, and therefore the computational costs to run the model are much less. However, it does maintain many of the dynamic features of a GCM and is a useful tool to explore the full probability density function of key parameters that have a large influence on the climate system. This in turn allows for a more comprehensive treatment of parametric uncertainty that is ignored or

underestimated when the IPCC GCM ensemble is used and, thus, provides more confidence that the uncertainty bounds around climate projections will contain the true climate-change pathway.

Methods

Earth Model of Intermediate Complexity

We will use the University of Victoria's ESCM to develop up to 100 model runs that simulate key climate parameters that affect temperature. This method helps to compensate for the truncated probability density function represented by the IPCC AOGCM ensemble, which does not fully sample the tails of the distribution. We will examine the impact of climate sensitivity, anthropogenic aerosol forcing, and ocean diffusivity on the climate system. These parameters have large effects on the global climate response. Climate sensitivity controls the total amount of CO_2 warming, aerosols are a large and most uncertain cooling forcing which may counterbalance some of the warming, and ocean diffusivity controls the rate of warming. The global responses of these parameters will in turn affect the regional climate change experienced in the Southeast. Our approach reduces the risk of overconfident decision making, because even though the probability is low that the realized future climate will track that of the less skillful EMIC runs, it is still a possibility. This possibility must be accounted for because of the potentially significant consequences for adaptation and mitigation.

The method to combine the EMIC uncertainty with the GCM uncertainty will depend on the outcome of the EMIC simulations. However, we will consider a number of possibilities. One possibility is to simply treat the EMIC like another GCM. This would conflate GCM uncertainties with EMIC uncertainties to produce projections that better characterize uncertainty relative to projections using GCMs alone. Another approach is to build a hierarchy of models where we treat the GCM ensembles as informing us about structural uncertainty, while the uncertainty across the EMIC runs represent purely parametric uncertainty. A third approach is to perform our inference in stages—to use the parametric uncertainty gleaned from the EMIC ensembles to "dress" the probability distributions of the variables based purely on the GCMs with appropriate "tails." By using the appropriate modeling approach, the resulting probability density functions will contain uncertainties derived from both GCMs and EMICs, representing both structural and parametric uncertainties.

Regardless of the method chosen, it will reflect our key motivation in the design of our analysis, namely that the tails of the projections, representing climate extremes, affect the decision-making problems addressed by the overarching project. The proposed method has the potential to improve representation of these tails by (1) adding another model structure (the EMIC) and (2) adding samples in the tails of the model parameters for the EMIC.

Statistically Downscaled Simulation

We propose to use a statistical-asynchronous regression approach to temperature downscaling, originally proposed by O'Brien and others (2001) and applied to climate projections by Dettinger and others (2004). The original methodology was modified to provide improved simulation of highly impact relevant extremes and tails of the daily temperature distribution. For precipitation, we propose to use a mixture model clustering approach including nonhomogeneous transition probabilities to model the occurrence and intensity of daily precipitation (Vrac and others, 2007). We will apply this dual-downscaling method to simulation output from 16 AOGCMs made available as part of the IPCC AR4 for projections to 2100. We will use long-term cooperative weather station locations in the Southeast from the U.S. Global Historic Climate Network (GHCN) for the observational training dataset and perform retrospective downscaling back to 1900. After applying this new downscaling approach to the GHCN weather station records in the Southeast, we will also consider applying these same methods to the gridded observations developed by Maurer and others (2002) as time and resources allow. Irrespective of this, we will provide gridded downscaled output at 1/8th degree resolution or higher (either as a direct output from the Maurer and others (2002) dataset or as a derived product from the GHCN station locations) for use by the other Southeast Regional Assessment Project research groups. Finally, we will extend the downscaling approach to

the ESCM runs to correct for model bias and to better approximate the full range of temperature values that are omitted due to the inability of the EMIC to resolve local scale processes. The final product will be over 100 regionally downscaled climate change projections (both EMIC and IPCC runs) of key climatic variables.

Bayesian Data-Model Fusion

We will apply Bayesian model averaging procedure (BMA; also known as "model dressing") (Draper, 1995; Hoeting and others, 1999) to the downscaled IPCC GCM and EMIC model ensembles to produce more accurate predictions of future climate across the Southeast while accounting for structural uncertainties across models, Bayesian prior uncertainties, and uncertainties introduced by downscaling the course global output to local levels. BMA calibration is a procedure for assigning probability weights to models based on how well they hindcast the observed climate. Models with better hindcast skill will receive higher weights. These weights can be used to produce a weighted average of a projected quantity in the context of a full probability density function (PDF). Historic climate data from the CDC and the NCEP will be used for the Bayesian calibration and weighting procedure. We will utilize state-of-the-art techniques for reducing the heavy matrix computations (Johanneson and Cressie, 2004; K.S. Bhat, [PSU], unpub. data, 2009), thereby allowing us to utilize all the data without resorting to currently often-used ad-hoc aggregation approaches.

Using a Bayesian statistical approach to estimate the final climate projections is advantageous because it provides a natural framework for deriving full probability density functions that represent the degree of confidence in our predictions. This enables a more comprehensive treatment of the structural uncertainty in projections resulting from the limited sample size of the GCMs. The procedure will also reduce predictive uncertainty because the data-model fusion will properly weight the climate projections according to how well the models reproduce historical observations. These data will then be used by other SERAP researchers to produce better projections of climate-derived products such as fire frequency, insect outbreaks, and water availability, either directly through the BMA weights or through the full probability distribution of the parameters of interest given by the data-model fusion.

Projections of Impact-Relevant Climate Indicators

The statistically downscaled probabilistic projections will be used to generate projections of changes in key climate indicators that have an important influence on ecosystem processes and species of interest. Impact-relevant climate indicators could consist of, for example, projected changes in consecutive days below freezing, drought intensity, and extreme heat days. The working list of variables is listed in table 1. Climate-derived products such as fire frequency and insect outbreaks are developed through a hindcast regression method, whereby a model is developed using climate parameters as a proxy for the variable of interest that is strongly influenced by climate (for example, fire frequency). Additional metrics to be used are determined in cooperation with the members of SERAP (who in turn are consulting with stakeholders in the FWS and partners in the Region 4 States). The probabilities obtained in the Bayesian data-model fusion step will be propagated to quantify climate uncertainty in the climate-derived products by more heavily weighting those impact projections driven by the more accurate climate models. North Carolina State University (NCSU) will also be responsible for coordination between all lead climate change analysis partners (NCSU, Pennsylvania State University (PSU), Texas Tech., and the USGS) and for rapid dissemination of climatic data to the aquatic and terrestrial teams.

References

Bernstein, L., Bosch, P., Canziani, O., Chen, Z., Christ, R., Davidson, O., Hare, W., Huq, S., Karoly, D., Kattsov, V., Kundzewicz, Z., Liu, J., Lohmann, U., Manning, M., Matsuno, T., Menne, B., Metz, B., Mirza, M., Nicholls, N., Nurse, L., Pachauri, R., Palutikof, J., Parry, M., Qin, D., Ravindranath, N., Reisinger, A., Ren, J., Riahi, K., Rosenzweig, C., Rusticucci, M., Schneider, S., Sokona, Y., Solomon, S., Stott, P., Stouffer, R., Sugiyama, T., Swart, R., Tirpak, D., Vogel, C. and Yohe, G., eds., 2008, Climate change 2007—Synthesis report: Contribution of Working Groups I, II and III to the Fourth Assessment Report of the Intergovernmental Panel on Climate Change, IPCC, Geneva, Switzerland, p. 104.

Dettinger, M., 2004, Simulated hydrologic response to climate variations and change in the Merced, Carson, and American River Basins, Sierra Nevada, California, 1900–2099: Climatic Change, v. 62, p. 283–317.

Draper, D., 1995, Assessment and propagation of model uncertainty: Journal of the Royal Statistical Society Series B-Methodological, v. 57, p. 45–97.

Hayhoe, K., Wake, C., Huntington, T. , Luo, L., Schwartz, M., Sheffield, J., Wood, E., Anderson, B., Bradbury, J., DeGaetano, A., Troy, T., and Wolfe, D., 2007, Past and future changes in climate and hydrological indicators in the U.S. Northeast: Climate Dynamics, v. 28, p. 381–407, DOI 10.1007/s00382-006-0187-8.

Hayhoe, K., Wake, C., Anderson, B., Liang, X.-L., Maurer, E., Zhu, J., Bradbury, J., DeGaetano, A., Stoner, A., and Wuebbles, D., 2008, Regional climate change projections for the Northeast USA: Mitigation and Adaptation Strategies for Global Change, v. 13, p. 425–436 (also available at *http://dx.doi.org/10.1007/s11027-007-9133-2*).

Hoeting, J.A., Madigan, D., Raftery, A., and Volinsky, C., 1999, Bayesian model averaging—A tutorial: Statistical Science, v. 14, p. 382–401.

Johanneson, G., and Cressie, N., 2004, Finding large-scale spatial trends in massive, global, environmental datasets: Environmetrics, v. 15, p. 1–44.

Jose, S., Jokela, E.J., and Miller, D.L., eds., 2006, The longleaf pine ecosystem—Ecology, Silviculture, and Restoration: New York, NY, Springer Science.

Maurer, E.P., Wood, A.W., Adam, J.C., Lettenmaier, D.P., and Nijssen, B., 2002, A long-term hydrologically-based data set of land surface fluxes and states for the conterminous United States: Journal of Climate, v. 15, p. 3237–3251.

Nakićenović, N, and others, 2000, IPCC Special Report on Emissions Scenarios: Cambridge, UK and New York, NY, Cambridge University Press.

O'Brien, T.P., Sornette, D., and McPherron, R.L., 2001, Statistical asynchronous regression— Determining the relationship between two quantities that are not measured simultaneously: Journal of Geophysical Research, v. 106, p. 13247–13259.

Schmittner, A., Urban, N.M., Keller, K., and Matthews, D., 2009, Using tracer observations to reduce the uncertainty of ocean diapycnal mixing and climate carbon-cycle projections: Global Biogeochemical Cycles, GB4009, doi:10.1029/2008GB003421.

U.S. Climate Change Science Program, 2009, Thresholds of climate change in ecosystems, synthesis and assessment product 4.2, 170 p.

Vrac, M., Stein, M., and Hayhoe, K., 2007, Statistical downscaling of precipitation through a nonhomogeneous stochastic weather typing approach: Climate Research, v. 34, p. 169–184.

Weaver, A.J., Eby, M., Kienast, M., and Saenko, O.A., 2007, Response of the Atlantic meridional overturning circulation to increasing atmospheric CO2—Sensitivity to mean climate state: Geophysical Research Letters, v. 34.

Wood, A., Leung, R., Sridhar, V., and Lettenmaier, D., 2004, Hydrologic implications of dynamical and statistical approaches to downscaling climate model outputs: Climatic Change, v. 62, p. 189–216.

Chapter II.   Integrated Coastal Assessment

By Nathaniel Plant, Glenn R. Guntenspergen, K. Van Wilson, Scott Wilson, Cindy Thatcher, Alexa McKerrow, and Adam Terando

Introduction

The IPCC (2007a) and the U.S. Global Change Research Program (USGCRP, 2009) have concluded that climate change is likely to intensify during the coming decades as a result of continued fossil fuel emissions and land-use change. As the temperature of the atmosphere increases, the volume of the world ocean is expected to increase due to thermal expansion of seawater and the melting of land ice (IPCC, 2007a). The rate of sea level rise during the past 15 years was approximately twice as high as the average rate observed globally over the past century (USGCRP, 2009). While the IPCC estimates of sea level rise through 2100 are in the range of 0.18 to 0.59 meters (m), several recent papers suggest that a 1 m or more rise in global mean sea level over the next century is plausible considering the current rates of sea-level rise and ice sheet decline (Rahmstorf 2007; Rahmstorf and others, 2007; Rohling and others, 2008; Vermeer and Rahmstorf, 2009).

Sea-level rise is among the most costly and most certain consequences of a warming climate (Scavia and others, 2002; Nicholls and others, 2007). Even with stringent climate-change mitigation (reduced greenhouse gas emissions), mean sea level will continue to rise for centuries due to the thermal inertia of the oceans and ice sheets and their long time scales for adjustments (IPCC, 2007a). As sea level rises, coastal shorelines will retreat and erode and low-lying areas will tend to be inundated more frequently, if not permanently, by the advancing sea. If tropical and extra-tropical storms increase in intensity, as projected by many studies (Emanuel 2005; Holland and Webster 2007; IPCC 2007a), shoreline retreat and wetland loss along low-lying coastal margins will accelerate further. Accelerated coastal retreat has already been observed in many tropical, mid-latitude, and Arctic regions (Nicholls and others, 2009). In addition to the conversion of land to open water, coastal retreat can diminish or eliminate many critical ecosystem services, such as support of commercially important fisheries, provision of wildlife habitat, improvement of water quality, and protection of human populations from storm surge and chronic tidal flooding.

Relative sea-level change at any coastal location is determined by the combination of eustasy (global sea-level rise) and local processes that affect elevation of the land surface, such as tectonism, isostasy (glacial rebound) and subsidence (sinking of the land surface due to sediment consolidation—a process that can be accelerated by oil, gas, and groundwater extraction; IPCC, 2007b). Subsidence is the predominant contributor to elevation change in the U.S. Gulf of Mexico coastal zone. Subsidence is highest in southeastern Louisiana, due to its geologic framework composed of recent deltaic deposits, and the region is affected by oil and gas extraction. Subsidence generally decreases westward and eastward of the Mississippi Delta. The western Mississippi coastline is experiencing higher subsidence rates than to the east in Alabama and Florida, but subsidence has been observed in the marshes of Grand Bay, MS (Schmid, 2001) and Mobile Bay, AL (Roach and others, 1987).

The South Atlantic and Gulf of Mexico coastal regions are prone to high rates of coastal erosion and flood disasters associated with hurricanes. Subsidence in some parts of the southeastern coastal plain serves to amplify the vulnerability of communities, infrastructure, and natural resources to storm-surge flooding. The Southeast Region ranks highest in the number of U.S. billion dollar weather-related disasters and flood insurance claims. The Gulf of Mexico coastal zone is already experiencing some of the highest rates of coastal erosion and wetland loss in the world. The high vulnerability of this low-lying coastal zone to land loss and flooding is generally attributed to the combined effects of human development activity, sea-level rise, hurricanes and other tropical storms, and a natural physical setting that is sensitive to subtle changes in the balance of marine, coastal, and onshore processes (Burkett, 2008).

In low-lying coastal areas where hurricanes are common, the prospect of an increase in mean sea level is of keen interest to decision makers. Emergency managers, developers, resource managers, and the general public in these vulnerable coastal regions need to know the potential impact of a rising sea level and how that phenomenon may influence plans for developing future critical infrastructure and for habitat restoration and conservation. Envisioning coastal change and identifying areas that are highly vulnerable to sea-level rise and erosion is a commonly cited need of coastal planners and natural resource agencies. Despite high awareness of global warming and moderately good understanding of potential impacts of climate change on coastal areas, currently pressing issues and limited staff time and resources constrain their ability to begin dealing with the growing risks from sea-level rise (Moser and Tribbia, 2007).

Improving the ability to predict future effects of sea-level rise on coasts is a major challenge for natural resource managers. For example, predicting changes in shoreline position and land loss resulting from erosion is difficult due to the complexity of coastal systems. This complexity arises from the wide range of variables and related feedbacks that influence responses to rising sea level, coupled with the interactive effects of human-development activities. In addition to uncertainties in future sea-level rise, there are also large uncertainties in predictions of future climate conditions (storms, for example) that drive the relevant physical and biological processes. To better support the management of coastal resources, more integrated assessments of sea-level rise and climatic change in coastal areas are required, including the significant non-climatic drivers (Nicholls and others, 2008).

This effort proposes to address the impacts of sea-level rise on coastal regions where inundation, land loss, and habitat change are expected to occur. As all three of these processes are related, we will address them in an integrated framework. The scope of the effort will be focused on the Mississippi and Alabama coastal areas where impacts from sea-level rise are likely to be substantial. The integration of the three processes (where we define inundation as the flooding of a static landscape, land loss as acting to change the landscape as a result of erosion or subsidence, and habitat change as the biologic response to the other two processes as well as other climatic drivers) will be achieved automatically through consideration of the natural spatial overlap of the processes and captured by observations, explicit numerical modeling, and statistical coupling. The outcome of the effort will be a succinct description of the interaction between sea-level rise and the landscape and habitat evolution and tools to estimate the likely response of this environment to predicted sea-level rise. Quantification of uncertainties will be an explicit part of the effort and will allow probabilistic risk assessments that are required to address coastal management problems.

Objectives and Approach

The overall goal of the coastal component of the NCCWSC SERAP is to demonstrate how the knowledge of coastal processes and sea-level rise, monitoring, and modeling can be integrated in a manner that supports coastal resource management. There are three primary objectives of the coastal component of SERAP:

- develop a Bayesian statistical framework that predicts coastal erosion and inundation under a range of sea-level rise scenarios and considers the combined effects of geologic constraints and other driving forces,

- assess the potential impacts of sea-level rise on coastal ecosystems and related wildlife resources, and

- develop visualization products that will help natural resource managers anticipate sea-level rise and adapt to the changes that are projected over the coming decades.

Objective 1—Land-Surface Elevation Changes

Task 1—Bayesian modeling of shoreline erosion

A Bayesian approach will be used to assess the potential for erosion and inundation in a study area that encompasses the coastal counties of Mississippi and Alabama. We will employ a Bayesian statistical framework that incorporates a wide range of geologic and oceanographic information about coastal systems, including uncertainties in physical properties and process characterizations, to make probabilistic predictions of the future state of coastal environments. Inputs to the prediction include datasets that provide information regarding the initial states of coastal systems, relevant forcing factors, historical observations, and model projections. Competing hypotheses for the forcing are used to drive the model, and resulting response scenarios and their uncertainties are compared. Initial results from the U.S. mid-Atlantic coastal region demonstrated this approach. These capabilities include risk analysis for decision support, providing a framework to engage decision makers and to help to define and address specific management questions related to sea-level rise. In addition, Bayesian analysis can also be used to prioritize research needed to reduce uncertainty in predictions.

Initially we will develop a Bayesian network for open ocean coastal response to sea-level rise using methods described above, which are similar to that used for the U.S. Atlantic (project funded by USGS Global Change Program). We will compare and contrast two available datasets for the Gulf of Mexico coast: (1) Thieler and Hammar-Klose (2000) 8-kilometer (km) resolution for Florida to Louisiana and (2) Pendleton and others (2003) 1-km resolution and new data from the USGS National Assessment of Coastal Change Hazards project for Gulf Islands National Seashore (and potentially Dauphin Island as well). The primary drivers that will be used to assess the potential for erosion along the Gulf of Mexico shoreline are coastal slope, geomorphic type, tidal range, mean wave height, and a range of plausible sea-level rise scenarios. We will also conduct an assessment of existing shoreline change assessment as a baseline predictor of future shoreline conditions and integrate results of the open ocean coastal effort with the project work described under the other coastal objectives and tasks.

Task 2—Direct observation of wetland elevations

Subsidence and vertical accretion rates in wetlands are two additional components that will be incorporated into the Bayesian network approach described above. These two variables are particularly important in determining inundation rates for areas that lie inland from the open Gulf Coast shoreline, where marine processes play a more important role in contemporary coastal evolution. Subsidence rates in the Mississippi/Alabama coastal region will be determined from three major sources: tide gages, elevation benchmarks, and Surface Elevation Tables (SETs). Data from tide gages and benchmarks are available from NOAA, though the available historical elevation data from benchmarks is generally confined to the vicinity of roads, airports, and other infrastructure. SETs are used to determine shallow rates of subsidence and vertical accretion at the land surface.

Vertical accretion rates are an important determinant of the sustainability of a coastal system as sea level rises. If accretion rates exceed the rate of sea-level rise, the land surface may not be inundated even if the rate of sea-level rise accelerates. The USGS has pioneered techniques for measuring vertical accretion at the soil surface in coastal marshes and forests. A critical component of this study is high-resolution measures of marsh surface-elevation change. The surface elevation table–marker horizon approach (fig. 1) makes it possible to quantitatively determine with high precision changes in marsh surface elevation, separate the contributions of surface and subsurface processes to surface elevation, calculate shallow subsidence (accretion minus elevation), and to partition shallow subsidence between shallow (root zone) and deeper (below the root zone to >10 m) portions of the soil profile using benchmarks of different depths. Vertical accretion (sediment deposition and erosion) is measured to the nearest millimeter from cores taken through soil marker horizons laid on the marsh surface (Cahoon and Turner, 1989). Surface-elevation change is measured from a SET (Cahoon and others, 2002), a highly precise (1–2 millimeter [mm]) mechanical leveling device that attaches to a benchmark driven into the substrate to refusal. SET measurements incorporate the surface processes measured from the marker horizon plus the subsurface processes occurring between the marker horizon and the base of the SET benchmark. The collective influence on surface elevation of these subsurface processes, which is called shallow subsidence, is calculated by subtracting elevation from accretion (Cahoon and others, 1995: fig. 1). A full and detailed explanation of the SET-marker horizon approach is provided at *http://www.pwrc.usgs.gov/set/*. Measures of elevation and accretion will be conducted seasonally over a 3-year period in the vicinity of each SET-marker horizon sampling station.

One year of data from the SETs will at least give a comparison of the rates of subsidence or accretion in the wetlands as compared to the leveling rates of vertical displacement of the National Geodetic Survey benchmarks. Once these SETs are installed, they can be used for data collection for future subsidence and accretion rate studies, as well as inputs to refine the Bayesian framework described in Task 1.

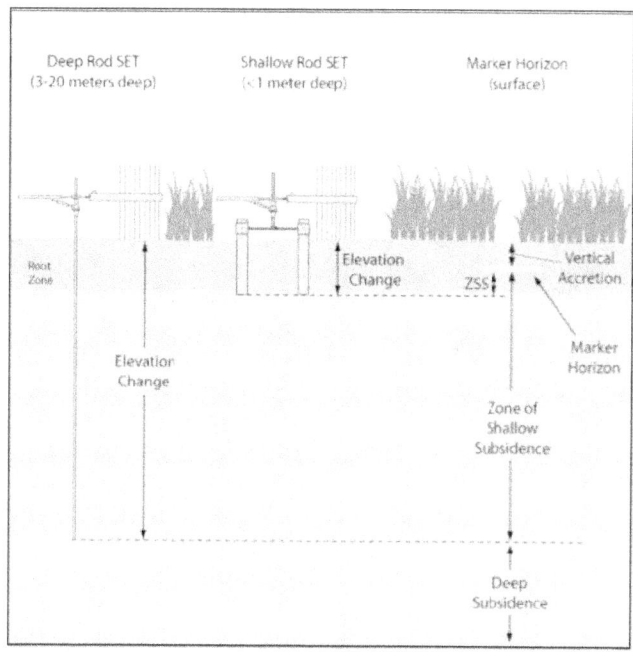

Figure 1.   Diagram showing the portions of the soil profile measured by deep and shallow rod Surface Elevation Table (SET) and marker horizon techniques, and deep and shallow zones of shallow subsidence.

Objective 2—Visualization

Partner agencies in the Southeast Region have placed high priority on tools that will help them visualize the impacts of climate change on resources they manage. The DOI manages an extensive network of coastal parks and refuges in the Gulf of Mexico and South Atlantic coastal zone. The DOI management agencies and several State fish and wildlife management agencies have already observed many changes in coastal areas that are consistent with effects projected for this region by the USGCRP (2009) and IPCC (2007b). Decision makers in natural resource and coastal management agencies are planning now and need tools and high-quality science information to prepare for and adapt to present and future impacts of climate change on coastal ecosystems.

We will develop a Google™ Thematic Mapper (TM) based map viewer that depicts inundation as sea level rises. This pilot project will be a collaborative effort with the NOAA Coastal Services Center and the USGS. The map-viewer application is based on a NOAA prototype that provides a user-friendly and familiar environment for resource managers and the general public to visualize the potential impacts of predicted sea-level rise. The interactive map viewer will allow the user to display elevations of 1 foot (ft), 3 ft, and 6 ft above the Mean Higher High Water datum, a tidal vertical datum referenced to local tides that is defined as the average of the daily higher high water height observed over the National Tidal Datum Epoch (NOAA, 2009). By referencing this datum, the sea-level-rise predictions are calculated as water levels would exist during an average high tide. Because rising sea levels will cause daily high tides to reach farther inland, this datum transformation is necessary to add an important tidal component to the inundation projections.

The Web mapping application will display sea-level rise inundation data developed by the USGS Mississippi Water Science Center, which is based on high-resolution Light Detection and Ranging (LiDAR) elevation data. One benefit to using these inundation data is that the data are available in the very near term, which allows us to meet the project timelines and public expectations relayed during a March 2009 stakeholder's meeting to discuss sea-level rise planning in Biloxi, MS. Additional sea-level rise and coastal habitat change projections developed using alternate methods can be included once they become available. For example, output from the Sea Level Rise Affecting Marshes Model (SLAMM) could be made publicly accessible through a Web-mapping application.

The map viewers can display traditional maps with roads and cultural features, high-resolution satellite data, or elevation data as the background layer. The sea-level-rise viewer will have added functionality such as the ability to change the transparency of the sea-level-rise data or to control the display (on/off) through a slider tool (seen in the far right side of the map in fig. 2). These tools will be designed to help the users orient themselves on the map and to provide a detailed spatial context to the sea-level-rise data. U.S. Census Bureau block-level population data will also be included as a background layer, which could help local planners identify locations where large numbers of residents are vulnerable to future sea-level rise. In addition, the sea-level-rise inundation map layers will be tiled and cached to increase Web-page loading speeds. Because the inundation maps will be developed at a very high horizontal resolution (3 m), caching will be necessary to speed the transfer of very large amounts of data.

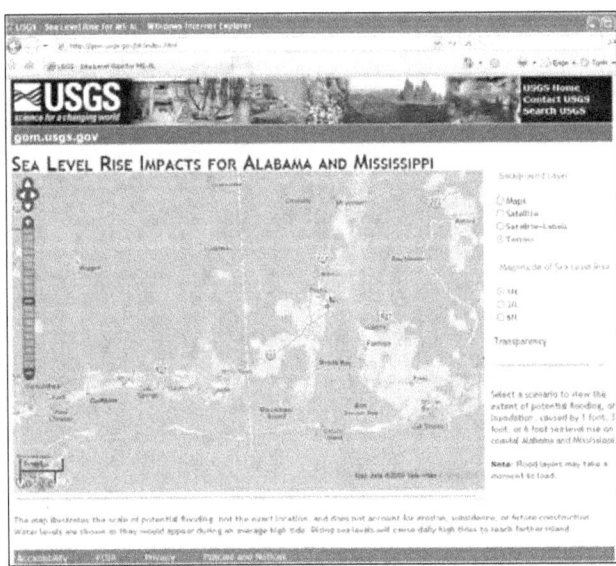

Figure 2.   A prototype version of a web-based sea level rise visualization tool for Alabama and Mississippi.

The prototype Web site (fig. 2) will be further developed with the addition of text and graphics. The Hurricane Katrina maximum storm tide data (Lavoie and others, 2008) for Alabama and Mississippi will also be added to the map-viewer application. Links to other climate-related studies will be provided, such as the Delaware Sea Level Rise Impact effort *http://csc-s-web-p.csc.noaa.gov/de_slr/*. The Web site will provide a summary of the methods used to develop the sea-level rise and storm-surge data, citations, and links to reports with detailed descriptions of the data.

This publicly accessible Web site will be located at *http://gom.usgs.gov/slr*. The site will be linked to the Gulf of Mexico Alliance as an example of a regional approach to climate change developed through a multi-agency partnership, which is one of the goals of the Governors' Action Plan (Gulf of Mexico Alliance, 2009).

Tasks:

- Develop a front-end interface. The front-end interface will be made using the JavaScript language and the OpenLayers library. Code must be written to lay out the OpenLayers map and map controls, enable special functionality such as the swipe tool, and access the map server.

- Develop back-end map server to serve the sea-level-rise data-map overlay. This server must be configured to serve the sea-level-rise data layers, which will be linked to OpenLayers controls in the front-end interface.

- Integrate the results of the land-surface-change tasks (Objective 1) in order to update inundation scenarios and provide visualizations of inundation and erosion risk.

- Integrate the results of the land-cover/habitat tasks (Objective 3).

- Optimize caching and layers for enhanced user performance.

- Develop an HTML Web site and add additional sea-level-rise related content.

- Migrate the visualization tool to public servers.

The sea-level-rise projections that will be developed during this project can be used to help answer important questions about potential impacts of climate change on key coastal infrastructure as well as the natural environment. We propose to conduct a Geographic Information System (GIS) analysis to identify infrastructure that would be inundated under sea-level-rise scenarios, such as transportation networks (for example, identifying sections of major roads that are projected to be flooded), railroads, airports, sewage treatment plants, power plants, military bases, and other elements of the built environment that are vital to society.

There may also be opportunities to integrate the results of this project with the USGS Northern Gulf of Mexico (NGOM) landscape and hazard forecasting project that is funded by the USGS Coastal and Marine Geology Program. The focus on the impacts of current and future coastal landscape changes on human populations is an important part of both projects (NGOM and SERAP) that could provide common ground for collaboration.

Objective 3—Ecosystem Changes

Sea-level rise is a significant regional climate change because of its possible effects on built, managed, and natural environments. While much focus is placed on the vulnerability of coastal systems specific to the threats to human interest, the goal of this task is to develop a methodology for assessing the potential impacts of sea-level rise on wildlife habitats. The physical and biological interactions spurred by sea-level rise are complex, with local processes being dictated not by a simple change in shoreline location ("a filling bathtub") but including processes such as saltwater intrusion, increased rates of erosion, and changes in deposition rates. The SLAMM (Park and others, 1986; Clough and Park 2008) attempts to identify coastal habitat change and land-surface loss through wetland conversion and shoreline modification. Much concern has been voiced about the validity of the SLAMM modeling approach and yet it is one of the tools currently available to help try to address the question of potential impacts of sea-level rise on habitats. To meet Objective 1 described in the previous section, USGS researchers will address the modeling needs to assess vulnerability of shorelines to erosion, to model and map sea-level-rise vulnerability and future sea-level-rise inundation, and to quantify the ecological processes that impact subsidence and accretion rates. Once the subsidence and accretion rate study is complete, the goal is to integrate that information into a detailed model to assess the impact of sea-level rise on habitats (vegetation) through time.

Given that context, we propose to complete the following three tasks:

- A rapid assessment of terrestrial vertebrate species due to habitat loss caused by sea-level rise for the coastal counties of Mississippi and Alabama.

- A detailed assessment of the sensitivity and accuracy of the SLAMM model results for a variety of geomorphic settings in the Southeastern United States.

- Collaboration with USGS and NOAA researchers to investigate the potential for expanding the current Bayesian modeling framework to predict habitat change through time.

Task 1—Rapid Assessment of Habitat Loss Due to Inundation

We plan to work with the output of the shoreline erosion and inundation vulnerability models to conduct a rapid assessment of projected species habitat loss due to inundation for the Mississippi and Alabama coastal counties. The Southeast Gap Analysis Program (GAP) has predicted distribution models for over 600 terrestrial vertebrate species that occur in the region (fig. 3) based on 2001 habitat availability. Future projections of inundation will be overlaid on those models to identify the extent and pattern of habitat loss. While not all species will be vulnerable to sea-level rise, some endemics or habitat specialists (for example, Loggerhead turtle, *Caretta caretta*) are likely to be highly vulnerable to changes in habitat availability due to sea-level rise. This assessment will provide a comprehensive regional list of those species.

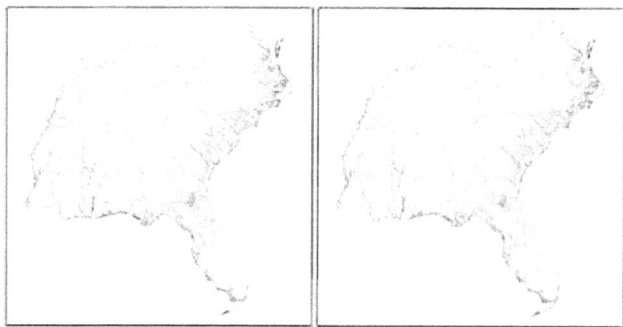

Figure 3. Map showing area covered by the Southeast GAP project.

Task 2—Assess the Sensitivity and Accuracy of the SLAMM Model

We will assess model performance by comparing historical shoreline change and coastal habitat type change to predicted values generated by the SLAMM model. We will use the earliest photo dates from the National Wetland Inventory as the baseline marker for the test sites. These photo dates range from 1977 to 1982 and will be compared to the most recent aerial photograph for the same sites (photo dates from the mid-1990s to the present). The photo comparison will be one primary output of the coastal assessment. The sensitivity of the model to vertical resolution of the input elevation data will be tested for a variety of sites using LiDAR or Interferometric Synthetic Aperture Radar (IFSAR) and National Elevation Data (NED). Finally, we will test the sensitivity of the model to the horizontal resolution of elevation data using LiDAR or IFSAR data. In addition, sensitivity of modeled outcome variability in accretion and erosion rates in the wetland classes at each of the test sites will help identify the relative importance of each of those parameters to the modeled outcome for each of the study sites.

Task 3—Collaborate with USGS and NOAA Researchers to Investigate the Potential for Expanding the Current Bayesian Modeling Framework to Predict Habitat Change Through Time

Key to this effort will be collaboration with researchers from both the USGS and others co-located with our research team in the North Carolina Cooperative Fish and Wildlife Research Unit who are developing a new Bayesian modeling framework to address the question of the impact of sea-level rise on habitat change for the Northeast and Mid-Atlantic coasts. We expect this proximity will allow for meaningful exchange of information and resources, thus leveraging the strengths of each team. Our research group has extensive experience in the development and application of regional datasets and a diversity of experts (for example, remote sensing, photo-interpretation, vegetation, vertebrate, and climate modeling) that would make expansion of the approach to the Southeast practical and efficient.

While this collaboration will need to evolve over time and guide the direction of this research, we have some ideas about the potential for building regional datasets that would provide historical patterns of land-cover change. Two existing datasets, the NOA) Coastal Change Analysis Project trends data for portions of the North Carolina coast and the land-cover trend data for the Louisiana coast developed by the National Wetlands Research Center could be used to test the expansion of the Bayesian modeling framework to include land cover change. If it is found that the historical record (1970–2005) are informative in projecting land-cover change due to sea-level rise, an effort to develop trends data for the entire Southeastern coast could be taken on at the end of the project. The NOAA Coastal Change Analysis Program is definitely interested in developing the coastal trends dataset for the entire U.S. coastline. This effort could serve to further strengthen the existing inter-agency partnership. If that research indicates the need for a longer time sequence, the aerial photography record could be used to extend the historical perspective of land-cover change through time.

As soon as the approach to modeling shoreline erosion and inundation (Objectives 1 and 2) can be expanded to include the coastline for the entire Southeastern coast, a rapid assessment of habitat vulnerability to sea-level rise for the >600 vertebrate species would provide State and regional wildlife agencies a triage list for species relative to the issue of sea-level rise. The next cycle of the State wildlife action plans are going to require that the States incorporate climate change in the planning process, making this a useful product to eight

of the States in the region. The outcome of the assessment of the SLAMM model will allow us to provide our partners with clear examples of the strengths and limitations of the approach specific to a range of geomorphic conditions in the Southeastern United States. It will also provide information specific to the datasets and parameters most likely to help in refining the projections, thereby helping prioritize future monitoring or data-gathering efforts. By working in parallel with the research team implementing the Bayesian modeling approach for the Northeast, we accelerate the delivery of high-quality modeling products for the Southeast Region. Once the Bayesian framework for modeling habitat change is built, the method could be used to provide a South Atlantic and East Gulf Coast-wide context analysis related to the loss of species habitat due to sea-level rise.

References

Burkett, V., 2008, The Northern Gulf of Mexico Coast: Human development patterns, declining ecosystems, and escalating vulnerability to storms and sea level rise, *in* MacCracken, M.C., Moore, F., and Topping, J.C., eds., Sudden and disruptive climate change—Its likelihood, character and significance: London, Earthscan Publications, p. 101–118.

Cahoon, D.R., Lynch, J.C., Hensel, P., Boumans, R., Perez, B.C., Segura, B., and Day, J.W., Jr., 2002, A device for high precision measurement of wetland sediment elevation—I. Recent improvements to the sedimentation-erosion-table: Journal of Sedimentary Research, v. 72, p. 730–733.

Cahoon, D.R., Reed, D.J., and Day, J.W., 1995, Estimating shallow subsidence in microtidal salt marshes of the southeastern United States—Kaye and Barghoorn revisited: Marine Geology, v. 128, p. 1–9

Cahoon, D. R., and Turner, R.E., 1989, Accretion and canal impacts in a rapidly subsiding wetland—II, Feldspar marker horizon techniques: Estuaries, v. 12, no. 4, p. 260–268.

Clough, J.S., and Park, R.A., 2008, SLAMM 5.0.1 technical documentation: Sea Level Affecting Marshes Model version 5.0.1, Warren Pinnacle Consulting, Inc, 38 p.

Emanuel, K., 2005, Increasing destructiveness of tropical cyclones over the past 30 years: Nature, v. 436, p. 686–688.

Gulf of Mexico Alliance, 2009, Governors' Action Plan II for Healthy and Resilient Coasts, accessed September 28, 2009, at *http://gulfofmexicoalliance.org/actionplan/welcome.html*.

Holland, G., and Webster, P., 2007, Heightened tropical cyclone activity in the North Atlantic—Natural variability or climate trend?: Philosophical Transactions of the Royal Society A, v. 365, p. 2695–2716.

Intergovernmental Panel on Climate Change, 2007a, Climate change 2007: The physical science basis, *in* Solomon, S., and others, eds., Contribution of Working Group I to the Fourth Assessment Report of the Intergovernmental Panel on Climate Change: Geneva, Switzerland.

Intergovernmental Panel on Climate Change, 2007b, Climate change 2007—Impacts, adaptation and vulnerability, *in* Solomon, S., and others, eds., Contribution of Working Group II to the Fourth Assessment Report of the Intergovernmental Panel on Climate Change: Geneva, Switzerland.

Lavoie, D.L, Rosen, B.H., Sumner, D.M., Haag, K.H., Tihansky, A.B, Boynton, Betsy, and Koenig, R.R., eds., 2008, USGS Gulf Coast Science Conference and Florida Integrated Science Center Meeting, *in* Proceedings with Abstracts, October 20-23, 2008, Orlando, Florida: U.S. Geological Survey Open-File Report 2008–1329, 157 p.

Moser, S.C., and Tribbia, J., 2007, Vulnerability to inundation and climate change impacts in California—Coastal managers' attitudes and perceptions: Marine Technology Society Journal, v. 40, no. 4, p. 35–44.

National Oceanic and Atmospheric Administration (NOAA), 2009, A Tutorial on Datums: accessed September 17, 2009, at *http://vdatum.noaa.gov/docs/datumtutorial.html*.

Nicholls, R.J., Wong, P.P., Burkett, V., Codignotto, J., Hay, J., McLean, R., Ragoonaden, S., and Woodroffe, C., 2007, Coastal systems and low-lying areas, *in* Climate change impacts, adaptations and vulnerability: Intergovernmental Panel on Climate Change Fourth Assessment Report, IPCC Secretariat, Geneva, Switzerland, p. 316–356.

Nicholls, R.J., Wong, P.P., Burkett, V., Woodroffe, C.D. and Hay, J., 2008, Climate change and coastal vulnerability assessment—Scenarios for integrated assessment: Sustainability Science, v. 3, no. 1, p. 89–102.

Nicholls, R. J., Woodroffe, C., and Burkett, V., 2009, Coastline degradation as an indicator of global change, *in* Letcher, T., ed., Climate change—Observed impacts on planet earth: Elsevier Press.

Park, R. A., Armentano, T.V., and Cloonan, C.L., 1986, Predicting the effects of sea level rise on coastal wetlands, *in* Titus, J.G., ed., Effects of changes in stratospheric ozone and global climate, v. 4—Sea level rise: U.S. Environmental Protection Agency, Washington, D.C. p. 129–152.

Pendleton, E.A.; Williams, S.J., and Thieler, E.R., 2003. Coastal vulnerability assessment of Fire Island National Seashore to sea-level rise: U.S. Geological Survey Open-File Report 03–439, 19 p.

Rahmstorf, S., 2007, A semi-empirical approach to projecting future sea-level rise: Science, v. 315, p. 368–370.

Rahmstorf, S., Cazenave, A., Church, J.A., Hansen, J.E., Keeling, R.F., Parker, D.E. and Somerville, R.C.J., 2007, Recent climate observations compared to projections: Science, v. 316, p. 709.

Roach, E.R., Watzin, M.C., Scurry, J.D., and Johnston, J.B., 1987, Wetland changes in coastal Alabama, *in* Lowery, T.A., ed., Symposium on the natural resources of the Mobile Bay Estuary, February 1987, Mobile, AL: Alabama Sea Grant Extension Service Publication No. MASGP-87-007. 208 p.

Rohling, E.J., Grant, K., Hemleben, C.H., Siddall, M., Hoogakker, B.A.A., Bolshaw, M., and Kucera, M., 2008, High rates of sea-level rise during the last interglacial period: Nature, v. 1, p. 38–42.

Scavia, D, Field, J.C., Boesch, D.F., Buddemeier, R.W., Cayan, D.R., Burkett, V., Fogarty, M., Harwell, M., Howarth, R., Mason, C., Reed, D.J., Royer, T.C., Sallenger, A.H., and Titus, J.G., 2002, Climate change impacts on U.S. coastal and marine ecosystems: Estuaries, v. 25, no. 2, p. 149–164.

Schmid, K., 2001, Shoreline erosion analysis of Grand Bay Marsh: Mississippi Department of Environmental Quality, Office of Geology, Jackson. 7 p.

Thieler, E.R., and Hammar-Klose, E.S., 2000, National assessment of coastal vulnerability to sea-level rise, U.S. Gulf of Mexico Coast: U.S. Geological Survey Open-File Report 00–179, 1 sheet.

U.S. Global Change Research Program, 2009, Global climate change impacts on the United States, *in* Karl, T.R., Melillo, J.M., and Peterson, T.C., eds.,: England, Cambridge University Press, 188 p.

Vermeer, M., and Rahmstorf, S., 2009. Global sea level linked to global temperature: Proceedings of the National Academy of Sciences, *http://dx.doi.org/10.1073/pnas.0907765106*.

Chapter III. Integrated Terrestrial Assessment

By Alexa McKerrow, Adam Terando, Steve G. Williams, Jaime A. Collazo, James Grand, James D. Nichols, J. Andrew Royle, and John R. Sauer

Introduction

We propose to develop a framework for using Adaptive Management (AM) and the principles of Strategic Habitat Conservation (SHC) to address the potential impacts of climate change on terrestrial and aquatic species in the Southeastern United States. AM provides an ideal framework for the establishment and attainment of conservation objectives in the face of tremendous uncertainty, while SHC is specifically designed to address issues associated with establishing and maintaining objectives related to populations of focal species. Although it can be argued that SHC is only applicable at landscape scales, the iterative nature of both processes is essentially parallel.

AM as defined in the U.S. Department of the Interior Technical Guide (Williams and others, 2007) involves assessment, design, implementation, monitoring, evaluation, and adjustment phases, while SHC requires biological planning, conservation design, implementation, monitoring, and applied research (USFWS, 2008). The assessment and design phases of AM are stakeholder driven and correspond closely with requirements associated with biological planning and conservation design—identification of focal species and their population status, development of population objectives, determination of habitat requirements, inventory of the available resources (habitat), determination of habitat objectives, and configuration of the desired landscape. These steps logically lead to the development of models that predict the results of conservation actions (that is, management or policy) referred to in SHC as decision-support tools. An emergent property of using either process in a structured decision-making context is the identification of fundamental objectives that describe the important outcomes of conservation actions, as well as the objectives that describe the actions themselves. This logically leads to the correct identification of the information necessary to understand the state of the system and the models necessary to predict the outcome of system dynamics resulting from changing environment or conservation actions.

AM is useful for addressing decisions related to climate change because it can be used to reduce structural and parametric uncertainty. Structural uncertainty refers to a lack of complete knowledge of the system (the environmental model). Thus, AM may be particularly well suited to decisions related to climate change, since there is great debate regarding nature of change and the effects on natural systems. Parametric uncertainty refers to the degree of response elicited by conservation implementation. Competing models are used to predict future system states as well as the nature and degree of species' response. Addressing both sources of uncertainty will require relatively precise predictions regarding the environment, the ensuing changes to the resources required by terrestrial species, and the effects of and responses to conservation actions. The monitoring programs required by AM and SHC are used to track progress toward objectives. Both types of uncertainty can be reduced through monitoring that addresses the key components and relations that define the system state. The identification of these key components is an emergent property of the process of describing system structure. The results of monitoring are used to identify and adapt the best performing system models and conservation actions. Thus, data and models that operate at increasingly finer scales, such as those proposed in the projects outlined here, will be required for us to learn how the system is evolving over time and whether conservation actions are leading to progress toward the stated objectives.

Central to our efforts is the development of new sources of data on environmental dynamics at sub-regional and local scales required by decision makers to predict responses of aquatic and terrestrial species. Land-use and land-cover data required to make strategic decisions for landscape design at various scales are becoming increasingly available, but models to identify and predict the effects of climate change on natural resources are required to inform decisions using potential future conditions. Combining information about historical climate and land-cover dynamics, large-scale studies, and monitoring programs of animal populations will provide the best opportunity to estimate responses to change. These estimates in turn can be used to project future change. One notable example of large-scale terrestrial species monitoring that can be scaled to make sub-regional and local predictions is the North American Breeding Bird Survey (BBS; fig. 1). However, these data are not without limitations,

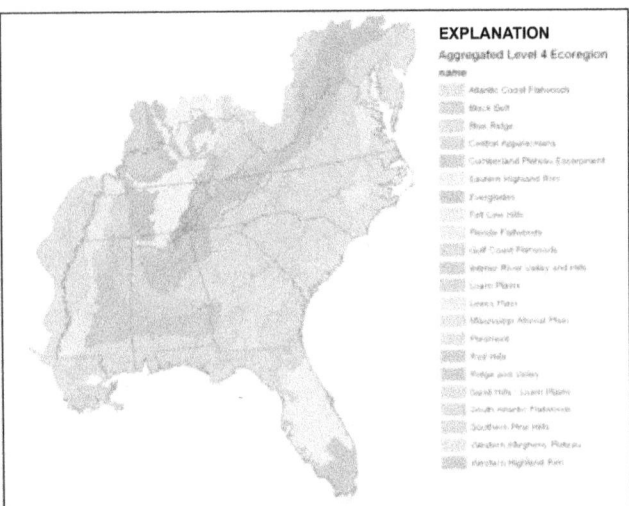

EXPLANATION

Aggregated Level 4 Ecoregion
name

Atlantic Coastal Flatwoods

Black Belt

Blue Ridge

Central Appalachians

Cumberland Plateau Escarpment

Eastern Highland Rim

Everglades

Fall Line Hills

Florida Flatwoods

Gulf Coast Flatwoods

Interior River Valley and Hills

Loam Plains

Loess Plains

Mississippi Alluvial Plain

Paristand

Red Hills

Ridge and Valley

Sand Hills - Loam Plains

South Atlantic Flatwoods

Southern Pine Hills

Western Allegheny Plateau

Western Highland Rim

Figure 1.   Proposed strata for sampling Breeding Bird Survey routes.

and techniques have only recently become available to use them to accurately and precisely estimate population dynamics parameters without the biases created by imperfect detection of animals on surveys. Using these new statistical techniques will make it possible to develop predictive models that address specific management objectives at relatively fine scales in areas that are strategically important to conservation, while concurrently seeking to improve and refine predictions about large-scale population dynamics in response to climatic and landscape changes. This is necessary because for this endeavor to succeed, we must predict, recommend, and monitor the results of management decisions for terrestrial wildlife populations at regionally meaningful scales, based on local management actions.

The complexity and geographic extent of the challenges in the Southeastern United States require not only an integrated project but also the expertise of many individuals, institutions, and partnerships to be successful and effective. Accordingly, we look forward to a close and sustained working relationship with the staff of the Southeast Regional Climate Science Centers, as well as with members of the emerging Adaptive Application Partnerships (AAPs) and LCCs, to ensure that research outputs are relevant and delivered to support and effect conservation of species and habitats at the appropriate spatial and temporal scales in the region.

Objectives and Approach

The overall goal of the SERAP is to develop a decision-making process that accounts for the uncertainty associated with predicting environmental dynamics and population responses, and the uncertainty associated with conservation policies and whether they will be effective. To meet this goal, we will address two objectives focusing on integrated terrestrial assessments:

- Assess potential impacts of climate change on habitats of priority species in the Southeastern United States by mapping and predicting land-cover dynamics,

- Assess patch occupancy and range dynamics of North American avian species in response to land-cover dynamics and climatic change in the Southeastern United States.

Objective 1—Assessing Potential Impacts of Climate Change on Priority Habitats

Modeling the future range of landscape conditions under a variety of policy and land-use scenarios is an effective way in which to provide managers the information they will need to adaptively manage for species. The research proposed here will provide the habitat dynamics models that will serve as the basis for a detailed regional assessment of priority species habitats. We will develop region-wide projections of urban growth and habitat dynamics models for priority species from 2001 to 2100. The work will be staged to provide urban growth and sea-level-rise models first and detailed habitat models later.

Task 1—Urban Growth Modeling

SLEUTH (Slope, Land use, Exclusion, Transportation, and Hillshade) uses cellular automaton modeling to predict the probability of each "cell" being developed through time (Clarke and Gaydos 1998; Clarke 2008). We will use the SLEUTH model within the USGS's Gigalopolis framework (*http://www.ncgia.ucsb.edu/projects/gig/*) to model spatially explicit urban growth throughout the study area. Five of the six input datasets needed are currently available through three USGS programs, specifically the NED (slope and hillshade), the National Land Cover Dataset (NLCD, general land cover and urban land use), and the National GAP (detailed land cover and land management and ownership). The sixth input dataset, the transportation corridors, is provided through the U.S. Census Bureau in the Topographically Integrated Geographic Encoding and Referencing (TIGER) system.

In order to calibrate the SLEUTH model, we will develop urban land-use maps for four dates (centered around 1992, 1996, 2001, and 2006). Candau (2002) found that calibrating with recent data (1963–1997) resulted in better performance than did models based on a long history (1929–1998) of training data. We will use the 2001 NLCD impervious surface dataset to train and estimate impervious surface from Landsat TM imagery for the remaining three dates. A threshold is then applied to the impervious surface estimates to classify urban categories consistent with the 2001 NLCD land-cover classification (open space developed, low, medium, high density urban; Homer and others, 2007). Four dates of roads coverage are created based on the TIGER road files for use in the calibration phase. We have found, based on our previous work, that filtering the urban data based on road density helps remove noise (scattered isolated urban pixels) and identifies urban areas that had been misclassified as non-urban due to high canopy closure in older, more established neighborhoods. The exclusion layer will be developed using the GAP Steward-ship and land-cover datasets. Public lands, private conserva-tion lands, and open water are excluded from development, while certain land-cover types (for example, wetlands) are assigned a lower probability of development.

Monte Carlo simulations are used in the calibration phase, and one of the fit statistics (Lee and Sallee or Compare) will be used to set the parameter (dispersion, breed, spread, and road growth) values for the final model runs. We are currently testing the model using the suite of fit statistics proposed in the literature (Jantz and others, 2009, Jantz and Goetz, 2005). The resulting dataset, probability of urbaniza-tion in yearly increments, will be used in conjunction with the sea-level and vegetation dynamics models to produce land-use and habitat maps for priority species from 2001 to 2100. For planning and reporting, an emphasis will be placed on the 2030 to 2050 time frame, the period when management and policy decisions put in place today are expected to start manifesting themselves on the landscape.

Task 2—Vegetation and Species Habitat Dynamics

We will use ESSA Technologies' vegetation dynamics modeling framework (TELSA in combination with VDDT) to derive spatially explicit probabilistic predictions of land-cover change through time. That framework relies on state transitions models to project the future condition of individual patches on the landscape. The transitions are Ecological System or land-cover type (for example, plantation pine) specific. The Nature Conservancy in collaboration with the LANDFIRE Interagency Project held a series of workshops for vegetation ecologists to populate those models. Experts were asked to identify the successional states for each vegeta-tion type and then to describe the probabilities and responses to a series of ecological processes (for example, succession, fire, insect outbreak). Those models in combination with the 2001 Southeast GAP land-cover map provide the basis for the vegetation dynamics modeling. For each patch in the landscape, the map is attributed with the initial condition (cover type, stage, and state). For this effort, we will use the Forest Inventory and Analysis data to obtain the initial stand structure characteristics for each of the forest types. For each time step (1 year) transitions are applied to each patch. A patch either succeeds to be a year older or a disturbance occurs and the state for that patch is changed. For example, if a patch of longleaf pine woodland has a surface fire, the understory would become "open."

The impact of climate change is currently incorporated in the vegetation dynamics model through a fire probability multiplier. The trend for the multiplier was determined by relating historical climate observation data with the area burned in each year in the South Atlantic Migratory Bird Ini-tiative (SAMBI) study area. That relationship is then applied to the projected climate in four IPCC scenarios (A1B, A2,

B1, and A1FI) to develop the trend line for fire probability for each one. Probability of a fire in each patch on the landscape is then determined by the current state of the patch, the original probability of a fire for that system in any one year, and the fire multiplier value for the time step being modeled.

In this project the regionally downscaled climate vari-ables, as well as the uncertainty projections being developed at PSU (Chapter I), will be incorporated to determine fire prob-abilities at a finer spatial resolution and to provide measures of the variability around those probabilities. Finally, climate projections will be used to model the potential impact of insect outbreak on vegetation dynamics. Currently the VDDT models include disturbances due to insects, but the potential for a change in the severity or extent due to insect population responses to changes in climate have not been modeled.

The resulting vegetation dynamics models provide yearly snapshots of the landscape condition, which can be used to model habitat availability using the habitat affinity models described below. These same landscape snapshots will be also be used as inputs into occupancy models for species in which sufficient observation data exist to develop estimates of species occupancy relative to landscape condition.

These landscape models will provide information for assessing the potential impact of climate change on the eco-logical systems of the Southeast Region. For example, if there are areas where fire frequency is projected to increase dramati-cally, that will have important implications for fire-dependent systems, as well as for the human population that co-exists. Indirectly these landscape models provide the basis for habitat models for priority species throughout the region.

Task 3—Habitat Models for Priority Species through 2100

In assessing the impacts of landscape change on priority species throughout the Southeast, we will employ a knowledge-based model approach utilizing habitat suitability indices (Schamberger and others, 1982). This approach allows us to incorporate species that do not have adequate sampling throughout the range of environmental conditions across the region. Relatively few species are well represented throughout their range with observation data; therefore we limit the modeling for many species to habitat affinity modeling so that they may be addressed in the context of conservation planning. The basis of the species habitat models will be taken from the recent Southeast GAP dataset. In that effort, species habitats were modeled on the basis of habitat preferences derived from literature and expert opinion compiled in a wildlife habitat relationship database. Models were then created in a GIS environment to produce a spatial representation of predicted habitat (Scott and others, 1993). In additional to species' use of land-cover map units, further restrictions were applied in the form of known range and other environmental factors that could be represented with remotely sensed data (for example, elevation, water affinity, anthropogenic disturbance; *http://www.basic.ncsu.edu/segap/downloads/SE-GAP%20 Ancillary%20Data%20Metadata.pdf*). This effort will expand on the presence or absence representation of GAP models by incorporating suitability rankings of habitat parameters through a series of workshops with biologists throughout the region. Each parameter will be identified as compensatory or limiting in nature, and the resulting spatial models will be depicted as a continuous surface.

The results of the first tasks (urbanization and vegetation dynamics models) are compiled to create a series of maps representing the projected landscape condition. At each time step, the landscape maps are then translated into a habitat suitability map for each of the priority species. Species maps can then be combined to project the priority areas for conservation through time.

These species models will directly inform the conservation planning and evaluation efforts at the Alabama Cooperative Fish and Wildlife Research Unit (CFWRU) (Objective 3). Projections based on a range of management and policy scenarios will provide stakeholders the ability to consider spatially explicit "what if" scenarios. The projected changes in habitat availability and pattern can then be used to assess the efficacy of actions (for example, restoration planting, land conservation) and policies toward meeting conservation objectives. The focal species, management objectives, and policy alternatives will be determined by stakeholders for each study area (ecoregion or watershed) in the series of workshops proposed Chapter V.

For example, in the South Atlantic coastal plain, the CRP provides landowner incentives for creating wildlife habitat on agricultural lands. The amount and distribution of incentives are determined by national- and State-level stakeholder groups. In a pilot project, models were developed to compare the opportunistic application of CRP to strategic allocation at the current level and double the current level. The strategic allocation was based on predictions of where restoration of wildlife habitat would have the greatest conservation benefit to grassland birds in the SAMBI area using projected changes in land cover. Additional scenarios and options will be determined on the basis of stakeholder (biologists and managers) feedback. Optimal solutions can then be determined on the basis of their expected contributions to meeting long-term conservation objectives.

Objective 2—Assess Patch and Range Dynamics of Avian Species in Response to Land Use Patterns and Climate Change

The goals of this project are to provide data on historical landscape conditions and estimate the recent (since 1970) rates of landscape change in the Southeast. These data will be useful for examining changes in the range dynamics of birds and other wildlife as they adapt to projected climate and habitat changes. The research proposed here seeks to estimate the rates of historical change in land use-land cover (LULC) in response to key climate parameters. Coupling climate-change data over the past 3 decades with large scale bird surveys (for example, the BBS) will permit inference about avian

responses to past change that can be used to develop models for projecting future avian responses. We expect that the approach developed here for avifauna can serve as a framework for other species and taxonomic groups as the necessary data are collected and organized. This effort will begin by specifying a priori hypotheses about avian change in response to changes in landscape and climatic changes. We will use recently developed occupancy models to estimate parameters associated with avian dynamics, while accounting for imperfect detection. As models are simultaneously developed for habitat responses to climate change, we will also describe avian dynamics in terms of habitat state changes as well as climatic change.

Task 1—Estimating Land Use Trends in the Southeast from 1970 to 2006

We will estimate the decadal rates of change among land-cover types at spatial and thematic resolutions necessary to estimate their relation to recent changes in the distribution of bird populations. Source imagery will be the North American Landscape Characterization (NALC) Triplicates, which contain Landsat Multispectral Scanner (MSS) images from 1973, 1986, and 1991. Although it has been argued that consistently accurate measurements of land-cover change can best be ensured using manual image interpretation (Sohl and others, 2004), manual interpretation of LULC change at the full spatial resolution of the data will not be feasible for the entire spatial scope of this project. Therefore, we will estimate rates of change on a stratified random sample of BBS routes, monitored over the same time period, using a combination of change vector analysis (McKerrow, 2007) and autologistic regression. The stratification will be based on an aggregation of Level 4 Ecoregions (see fig. 2) (Omernik 1987, 1995), and the land-cover classification will be based on a modified Anderson Level 2 legend. The finer stratification and greater thematic resolution more accurately represent avian (wildlife) distributions. The probability of transition among land-cover types will be estimated in relation to climatic data using autologistic regression.

Independent variables for the estimators will be based on a priori hypotheses regarding the factors that influence change from one class to another. For example, the probability change from mixed forest to other classes (for example, evergreen forest) within the eastern portions of the Southeast Coastal Plain ecoregion may be influenced by anthropogenic factors related to regional land-use practices or changes in temperature and precipitation. Competing models will be evaluated based on multinomial maximum likelihood estimators employing link functions to estimate the odds of change based on ancillary datasets (proximity to population centers and transportation corridors [anthropogenic] or frequency and severity of drought [climatologic]). The final result will be estimates of the rates of change among LULC classes, as well as the best approximating models relating climatic and anthropogenic factors to observed change.

Task 2 – Modeling the Impact of Land Use and Climate Change on Avian Species Occupancy

We will quantify processes underlying current avian distribution patterns and predict potential for sustaining populations based on patch occupancy dynamics and projected land-use change and climate in the South Atlantic Coastal Plain; additionally, we will quantify responses of ecosystem components (North American landbirds) to recent climate variation and change. Specifically, we will test hypotheses about recent changes in species ranges corresponding to climate change during the last 3 decades in the Southeastern United States and develop models predicting future range dynamics in response to predicted climate change in the Southeastern United States.

We will use occupancy models to discern processes behind occurrence patterns of avian species in response to observed changes in habitat at landscape levels in the South-eastern United States (MacKenzie and others, 2006). At the core of this effort will be BBS data and remotely sensed data. The first set of analyses will build upon the work in the South Atlantic Coastal Plain using data from 1992 to 2001. Inferences about species-habitat relationships will be at the NLCD level, since this is the classification level that will be used for the historical assessment of LULC (1973–2006). Further analyses will focus on the 2001 land-cover classification (Southeast GAP), which permits assessing relations to plant communities that are deemed optimal, suitable, or marginal for many land birds (Hamel, 1992). For this particular set of analyses, BBS routes will be divided into four segments of 5.6 km, separated by 4.8 km. The motivation for this approach is to better relate the approximate location of count stations along a route and mapped habitat. Shorter routes also reduce habitat heterogeneity by two to three classes. The eight stops per segments are treated as sampling replicates permitting estimation of species-specific detection probabilities. Failure to deal adequately with detection probabilities is an important shortcoming of the vast majority of macro-ecological research. Candidate set models (a priori hypotheses) will be formulated on the basis of a species' life history and habitat requirements, an effort aimed at capturing the species' ecological (landscape) basis for sensitivity. Processes (patch dynamics) and inferences about "sustainability" will be derived from relations between habitat and expressions of rates of extinction and colonization. We will use single-season and a combination of multi-season and integrated habitat-occupancy models to conduct analyses. The latter two modeling frameworks will allow incorporating habitat change and climate indicators as covariates to discern the processes of interest (such as colonization and extinction rates).

BBS data will also be used to assess range dynamics of selected species. Species selection will be based on BBS data since 1973, provided they are reasonably well sampled and we can develop general range maps. We will define near-boundary locations as those falling within some specified distance of the boundary (likely some multiple of BBS route length; for example, either 40 or 80 km). For each selected species, we will use multi-season occupancy modeling (see, MacKenzie and others, 2003, 2006), in conjunction with the BBS data, consisting of counts on each of 50 stops on each route. The parameters of biological interest, local probabilities of extinction, colonization, and occupancy, will be modeled as functions of route location within the species range, with competing hypotheses represented by different constraints on location-specific parameters. We plan to use an autologistic function in which patch dynamic-parameters (local extinction, colonization, occupancy) are modeled as possible functions of occupancy of neighboring locations. This modeling is made difficult by the fact that occupancy of neighboring locations is not known, either because locations are not sampled (no BBS route) or because sampling yields no detections (BBS route is present but the species is not detected there). Because of imperfect detection, nondetection is an ambiguous event that can result from either true absence of the species or presence but nondetection. The inference approach that we will likely use (see below) permits prediction of occupancy status of neighboring locations, thus providing a basis for inference about neighborhood effects. Model selection approaches will be used to decide on the most useful models, and the estimated signs, magnitudes, and variances of model coefficients will be used to judge degree of correspondence of estimates with hypothesis-based predictions. The second set of hypotheses about decadal changes will use similar modeling as above with the addition of parameters describing the rates of change in probabilities of local extinction and colonization at different locations. We can use either likelihood-based approaches or Markov Chain Monte Carlo Bayesian approaches to model fitting and estimation and will likely opt for the latter approach. In addition to providing a good approach for dealing with the autologistic modeling (which would be more difficult to implement with a frequentist approach), the Bayesian approach provides a natural framework for mapping based on current and projected (using decadal models) range dynamics (see Kery and others, 2005; Royle and others, 2005).

Three focal species have been selected for preliminary occupancy-habitat analyses and model development, as needed. These are the Brown-headed Nuthatch, Carolina Chickadee, and Summer Tanager. These species are south-centric in distribution to facilitate exploring hypotheses regarding the interplay between habitat and climate at the center but also at the fringe of their distributions. Once models are fully developed and tested, we anticipate that 30–50 species of landbirds in the Southeast could be analyzed following the same protocols resulting from this work. In addition to understanding and predicting potential consequences stemming from climate change, model outputs could be used to validate underlying assumptions about biological processes incorporated in knowledge-driven models (see Objective 1, Task 3).

References

Candau, J.C., 2002, Temporal calibration sensitivity of the SLEUTH urban growth model: University of California, Santa Barbara, M.A. thesis.

Clarke, K.C., 2008, Mapping and modelling land use change: An application of the SLEUTH model, *in* Pettit, C., Cartwright, W., Bishop, I., Lowell, K., Pullar, D., and Duncan, D., eds., Landscape analysis and visualization: Springer, p. 353–366.

Clarke, K.C., and Gaydos, L., 1998, Long term urban growth prediction using a cellular automaton model and GIS—Applications in San Francisco and Washington/Baltimore: International Journal of Geographical Information Science.

Conroy, M.J., and Noon, B.R., 1996, Mapping of species richness for conservation of biological diversity—Conceptual and methodological issues: Ecological Applications, v. 6, p. 763–773.

ESSA Technologies Ltd., 2007, Vegetation dynamics development tool user guide, version 6.0: ESSA Technologies Ltd., Vancouver, BC, 196 p.

Hamel, P.B., 1992, The land manager's guide to the birds of the South: Chapel Hill, NC, The Nature Conservancy, Southeastern Region. 437 p.

Jantz, C.A., and Goetz, S.J., 2005, Analysis of scale dependencies in an urban land-use-change model: International Journal of Geographic Information Science, v. 19, no. 2, p. 217–241.

Kery, M., Royle, J.A., and Schmid, H., 2005, Modeling avian abundance from replicated counts using binomial mixture models: Ecological Applications, v. 1, no. 5, p. 1450–1461.

Lambeck, R.J., 1997, Focal species: A multi-species umbrella for nature conservation: Conservation Biology, v. 11, no. 4, p. 849–856.

Mackenzie, D.I., Nichols, J.D., Hines, J.E., Knutson, M.G., and Franklin, A.B., 2003, Estimating site occupancy, colonization and local extinction probabilities when a species is not detected with certainty: Ecology, v. 84, p. 2200–2207.

Mackenzie, D.I., Nichols, J.D., Royle, J.A., Pollock, K.H., Bailey, L.A., and Hines, J.E., 2006, Occupancy modeling and estimation: San Diego, CA, Academic Press, 324 p.

Marcot, B.G., Steventon, J.D., Sutherland, G.D., and McCann, R.K., 2006, Guidelines for developing and updating Bayesian belief networks applied to ecological modeling and conservation: Canadian Journal of Forest Research, v. 36, p. 3063–3074.

McKerrow, A.J., 2007, Mapping and monitoring plant communities in the Coastal Plain of North Carolina—A basis for conservation planning: North Carolina State University, dissertation, 196 p.

Nyberg, J.B., Marcot, B.G., and Sulyma, R., 2006, Using Bayesian belief networks in adaptive management: Canadian Journal of Forest Research, v. 36, p. 3104–3116.

Omernik, J.M., 1987, Ecoregions of the conterminous United States: Annals of the Association of American Geographers, v. 77, p. 118–125.

Omernik, J.M., 1995, Ecoregions—A spatial framework for environmental management, *in* Davis, W.S., and Simon, T.P., eds., Biological assessment and criteria—Tools for water resource planning and decision making: Boca Raton, FL, Lewis Publishers, p. 49–62.

Royle, J.A., Nichols, J.D., and Kery, M., 2005, Modeling occurrence and abundance of species when detection is imperfect: Oikos, v. 110, p. 353–359.

Schamberger, M., Farmer, A.H., and Terrell, J.W., 1982, Habitat suitability index models— Introduction: FWS/OBS-82/10, Washington, D.C., U.S. Department of the Interior, U.S. Fish and Wildlife Service, Office of Biological Services and Division of Ecological Services.

Scott, J.M., Davis, F., Csuti, B., Noss, R., Butterfield, B., Groves, C., Anderson, H., Caicco, S., D'erchia, F., Edwards, T.C., Jr., Ulliman, J., and Wright, R.G., 1993, Gap analysis—A geographic approach to protection of biological diversity: Wildlife Monographs, v. 123, p. 1–41.

Sohl, T.L., Gallant, A., and Loveland T., 2004, The characteristics and interpretability of land surface change and implications for project design: Photogrammetric Engineering and Remote Sensing, v. 70, no. 4, p. 439–448.

U.S. Fish and Wildlife Service, 2008, Strategic habitat conservation handbook—A guide to implementing the technical elements of strategic habitat conservation (version 1.0): National Technical Assistance Team, U.S. Fish and Wildlife Service, Washington, DC.

Williams, B.K., Szaro, R.C., and Shapiro, C.D., 2007, Adaptive management—The U.S. Department of the Interior Technical Guide: Adaptive Management Working Group, U.S. Department of the Interior, Washington, DC.

Chapter IV.   Multi-Resolution Assessment of Potential Climate Change Effects on Biological Resources: Aquatic and Hydrologic Dynamics

By James Peterson, Lauren Hay, Kenneth Odom, W. Brian Hughes, Robert Jacobson, John Jones, and Mary Freeman

Introduction

This component of the SERAP will develop information and modeling approaches to help resource managers assess potential effects of climate change on biological resources. The specific focus of this research is on aquatic biota, especially freshwater fishes and mussels, and on improving our ability to answer questions concerning how species are likely to respond to climate-induced hydrologic change.

This research has two interrelated objectives. One is to develop tools that wildlife resource managers can use to predict climate-change effects across large regions and at local landscape scales. The appropriate resolution for analyzing the effects of climate change will differ depending on the scope of the resource question and the limits of potential management actions (for example, from regions or ecoregions to local landscapes that support particular species of concern). Thus, a multi-resolution approach to understanding and predicting climate-change effects on wildlife and other ecological resources will be essential for developing effective and cost-efficient conservation strategies. Our first objective is to develop modeling approaches to assess climate-change effects on aquatic biota at two spatial extents and two levels of resolution, each with specific management questions, response units, data requirements, and associated costs (fig. 1). For each level of resolution, we will work with resource managers to identify key management questions and objectives and to conceptualize links between climate change, wildlife resources, and management actions.

Our second objective is to evaluate how the choice of model resolution affects assessment of ecological sensitivity to changes in climate, hydrology, land-cover dynamics, surface-water dynamics, and land use. Assessments are often made at relatively coarse scales of resolution; for example, as in initial evaluations of potential effects of land use or climate trends on wildlife over large geographic areas. However, the processes that link climate, land cover, and management to wildlife

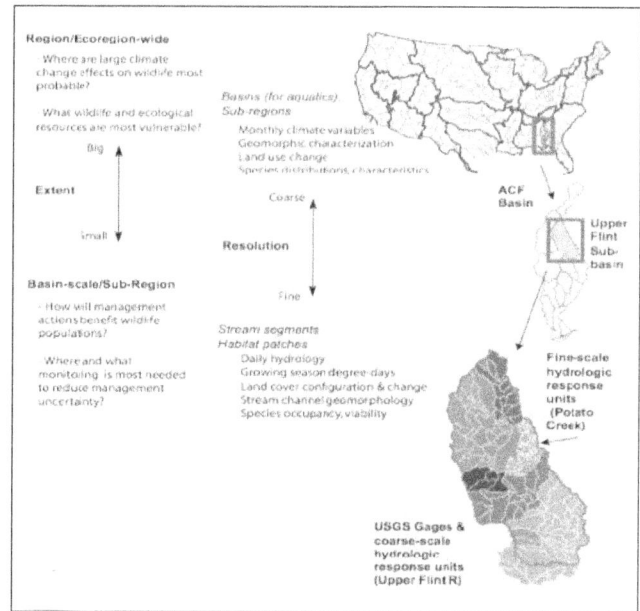

Figure 1. A graphical representation of the proposed multi-resolution approach for assessing climate change effects on ecological resources. [ACF, Apalachicola–Chattahoochee–Flint]

resources frequently occur at finer spatial scales than may be captured by coarse-scale assessments (hydrologic alteration in specific river reaches that support imperiled species; strategic conservation of population source habitats). Conversely, conditions characterized at larger spatial scales frequently set boundary conditions for local landscapes, as in isolation of headwater rivers by downstream dams, for example. It is, thus, particularly important for designing future assessment methods that researchers and managers understand changes in the information content of differing measures of ecological, hydrologic, terrain, and geomorphic characteristics in relation to changes in measurement scale.

Phase I of the project will develop and demonstrate a multi-resolution approach to assessment in the context of the Apalachicola-Chattahoochee-Flint (ACF) River Basin, chosen because the basin supports multiple fish and wildlife species of conservation concern to federal and State managers, is regionally important for water supply, and has been a recent focus of complementary research, providing an empirical basis for tool development. Using probabilistic projections of climate change developed for this integrated assessment, we will model effects on aquatic biota at coarse (the entire ACF Basin) to fine (stream networks within the ACF Basin) resolutions, providing estimates of biological responses for alternative climate scenarios and, at finer resolutions, potential management actions. Early in Phase I, we will consult with regional resource managers to identify priority biological management objectives and potential management actions in response to climate change. In Phase II, researchers will confer with resource managers to examine usefulness of coarse- and fine-resolution models for supporting biological planning and conservation design, as defined under Strategic Habitat Conservation, and to explore how the appropriate model resolution may depend on characteristics of species, landscapes, and limiting factors. Understanding and models developed in Phase I will then be used to identify species and ecoregional areas that are especially vulnerable to projected climate-change effects, to develop models at appropriate resolutions for those species (terrestrial and aquatic), and to design data-collection strategies that will address the largest sources of uncertainty identified in Phase I.

Methods

Our approach is based on the understanding that water availability and aquatic species dynamics are largely influenced by precipitation and temperature as modified by the landscape and geomorphic factors that influence runoff, sediment delivery, and stream morphology. Thus, understanding and predicting potential climate-change effects on the distribution and dynamics of aquatic species, and on water availability for human needs, will require integrating hydrology and land-cover dynamics across the geomorphic template that forms aquatic habitat, and then interpreting projected changes in terms of species responses to alternative management actions.

Project scientists will develop models for linking hydrology and land cover to aquatic species at basin to stream-segment levels of resolution, to support decision needs at regional to local levels (see fig. 1). These models will be loosely coupled through use of the Web-based data service being developed by the USGS North Carolina Cooperative Fish and Wildlife Research Unit. In addition to the dissemination of nationally downscaled climate-change datasets, this Web service will be used to facilitate dissemination of our model inputs and outputs. Component models and approaches are described below, followed by procedures for predicting species responses at coarse and fine resolution.

Phase I—Component Models

Hydrologic modeling structure. Hydrologic models will be developed using the Precipitation Runoff Modeling System (PRMS; Leavesley and others, 1983; Hay and Umemoto 2007). PRMS (1) simulates land-surface hydrologic processes including evapotranspiration, runoff, infiltration, and interflow estimated by balancing energy and mass budgets of the plant canopy, snowpack, and soil zone on the basis of distributed climate information (temperature, precipitation, and solar radiation); (2) simulates hydrologic water budgets at the watershed scale with temporal scale ranging from days to centuries; and (3) integrates with models used for natural-resource management or other scientific disciplines. For the ACF application, PRMS will require research and development of new multi-resolution capabilities. This new development in PRMS will provide methods for addressing multiple spatial extents and resolutions within a single model structure and will support a variety of temporal simulation contexts (historic, current, and future).

Daily time-step PRMS models will be developed at spatial scales corresponding to (1) major "subbasins" (approximately 8-digit Hydrologic Unit Codes) within the ACF, (2) streamgage locations (nested within subbasins), (3) coarse-scale response units (nested within watersheds defined by streamgage locations), and (4) fine-scale response units corresponding to stream segments (fig. 1). Models for subbasins will be used in coarse-resolution assessments; the smallest two levels of resolution (coarse-scale and fine-scale response units) will be appropriate for modeling species occupancy dynamics, explained below. For the fine-scale response units, pilot models of stream temperature (using, for example, the Stream Network Temperature model, SNTEMP) will be developed to allow investigation of the potential magnitude of change in seasonal stream-temperature patterns under climate-change scenarios.

PRMS simulations for future conditions at each resolution will be facilitated through use of the Web-based data service being developed by the USGS North Carolina Cooperative Fish and Wildlife Research Unit. This will contain the downscaled GCM information needed to run PRMS. Urbanization and land-cover projections developed by the other research teams and incorporated into the Web-based data service will be used in conjunction with the downscaled GCM output to produce the future PRMS projections.

Geomorphic characterization and stream channel classification. Geomorphic models will be developed for coarse and fine resolutions to characterize variation in (1) basin topography, using conventional digital elevation model (DEM) data and, for a subbasin within the ACF, high-resolution LiDAR, and field data; and (2) channel network structure and controls on the spatial distribution of persistent habitat features (deep pools, bedrock riffles, bedrock-constricted reaches) that influence colonization by fishes and other aquatic biota. At the stream-network scale, models will be developed for predicting ecologically relevant channel-morphology classes, for use in species-occupancy models. We hypothesize that channel form and bed-sediment composition can be used to describe ecologically distinct stream classes that differ in how flow variation affects habitat and population processes. We will, thus, develop and test models for classifying stream segments according to form (relative width and depth dimensions) and sediment (accumulation of fine alluvium) from remotely sensed topographic data. Regional classifications developed from coarse-scale data will be compared with basin-scale classifications developed from fine-scale data, and with field-based measurements, to assess information content/cost ratios over multiple scales and resolutions.

Terrain characterization, and land cover and surface water dynamics. Multi-resolution landscape dynamics databases including latent heat, biomass indices and multiple indices of land-cover "disturbances," and surface-water body size and distribution will be developed using TM/ETM+ (enhanced thematic mapper plus scanner) scenes spanning 1983–2008, a revised Advanced Very High Resolution Radiometer (AVHRR) vegetation index database for 1989–2006, and atmospherically calibrated Landsat scenes. Deriving and analyzing pertinent landscape variables from remotely sensed data allows the use of vegetation and surface-water dynamics to improve hydrologic models (Viger and others, 2010). These data also support direct measures of rates of change in land cover and extent of surface water (wetlands and constructed storage), used in turn to relate effects of climate, land use, and hydrologic dynamics on riparian communities. Derived variables will include subwatershed flow retention (through reservoir and storm pond survey), land-change frequency analysis, spatially distributed evapotranspiration modeling, and floodplain vegetation dynamics. As above, landscape and surface-water dynamics estimated for larger scales from fine-resolution assessments will be compared to equivalent estimates based on coarse-resolution data to investigate influence of resolution on information content.

Species response models. To support large-extent, coarse-resolution assessment, we will develop models that use species characteristics (reproductive traits, dispersal abilities, habitat affinities) to predict species vulnerability to changes in differing climate variables provided by the probabilistic projections of climate change. Species-specific distributions for freshwater fishes and mussels within the ACF will be mapped at coarse resolutions from available databases (Brim Box and Williams, 2000; Georgia Museum of Natural History). Species traits will be assigned from published and unpublished datasets. Coarse-scale assessments will target fish and mussel species that are identified as "priority targets" by regional FWS and State resource managers.

For fine-resolution assessment, we will develop multistate, multi-season occupancy models to project species occurrences at a stream segment scale for two subbasins within the ACF, the Piedmont and Coastal Plain portions of the Flint River Basin. These two subbasins are of interest because they support federally listed species of unionid mussels as well as species-rich fish assemblages within stream networks that are minimally influenced by large reservoirs. Thus, each of these subbasins is considered important to long-term conservation of native biological diversity. Models will permit comparisons of simulated responses by fishes and mussels to projected climate changes between Piedmont and Coastal Plain settings.

Assessing Climate Change Effects on Biota

Coarse-resolution approaches. We will develop two modeling approaches, expert judgment and empirical simulation, for assessing the response of aquatic biota to climate change at the coarse level. One objective will be to identify distinct costs and benefits for each approach in order to help inform choices of how to conduct coarse-level assessments across the region. We will initiate the process by conferring with regional FWS and State resource managers in a facilitated workshop to identify priority species targets, management objectives, and decision alternatives appropriate to differing levels of resolution. This workshop will be conducted early in the overall project, and in collaboration with the team modeling climate-change effects on bird habitat dynamics to allow the managers and researchers to explore areas where aquatic and terrestrial management objectives and decision alternatives overlap.

The expert judgment approach will be similar to that used by the U.S. Department of Agriculture Forest Service to evaluate the response of stream habitats and salmonids to alternative land management strategies in the Pacific Northwest (Reiman and others, 2001). We will assemble an expert team of aquatic ecologists, physical scientists, and resource managers familiar with the ACF system that will develop a conceptual model of the expected response of the priority species targets to changes in climate, accounting for geomorphic characteristics, landscape dynamics, system fragmentation, and other relevant features identified by the expert team. To allow the models to be applied to coarse-resolution landscape units with different species pools, the model will focus on predicting the response of species based on life history characteristics (reproductive strategies, dispersal abilities). The conceptual models will be parameterized using information from published studies, existing (unpublished) data, and expert judgment. Climate-change effects on priority species targets throughout the ACF Basin will then be assessed using outputs from hydrologic, terrain, and stream geomorphic models. For example, coarse-level projections of monthly discharge and other flow variables identified by the expert team as likely drivers of species persistence will be extracted for ACF subbasins from PRMS models, under differing probabilistic climate-change projections. Similarly, geomorphic (mean channel slope, occurrence of bedrock shoals, system fragmentation) and land use-land cover characteristics will be summarized for subbasins, for those variables identified as drivers in the coarse-resolution models.

We anticipate that the expert judgment approach will be the most feasible coarse-level approach to apply across a large and diverse region, such as the Southeast. However, the model will not be directly linked with fine-resolution models, which could complicate stepping-down assessment results to support decision making at resolutions relevant to local populations. To directly link the fine-resolution (described below) and coarse-resolution approaches, we will develop models for estimating changes in aquatic species distribution and persistence at the subbasin scale, using the inputs and predictions from the fine-scale simulation modeling. Summary indices of projected changes to the climate and landscapes at the subbasin scale will be calculated from the corresponding fine-scale estimates. For example, changes in the timing or frequency of high flows will be calculated from annual summaries of seasonal high-flow estimates from fine-resolution hydrologic models (an input to the fine-scale ecological response models). Similarly, outputs from the fine-scale ecological response models (stream-segment occupancy rates) will be summarized at coarser scales. We will then relate the simulated coarse-level changes in the biota to the predicted coarse-level changes in inputs to the fine-scale model (discharge, temperature, land change) using hierarchical models (Bryk and Raudenbush, 2002). Similar to the expert judgment modeling approach, we will use life history characteristics of the species to inform the species response models.

Fine-resolution approach. Our fine-resolution models are based on the assumption that at relatively large spatial extents and long timeframes, the dynamics of stream-dwelling populations primarily consists of the extirpation (or persistence), colonization, and reproduction of local populations. Thus, our fine-resolution approach will model the response of fish and mussel populations to discharge, temperature, landscape dynamics, and stream geomorphic characteristics using stochastic, multi-state stream-segment occupancy models. The models will simulate the colonization, reproduction, and persistence dynamics of individual species in stream segments. The occupancy models will operate on an annual time step with initial species presence randomly assigned to each segment using existing species-presence models (Ruiz and Peterson, 2007). During each time step, species-specific colonization, reproduction, and extinction probabilities will be estimated as functions of discharge, temperature, geomorphic stream-segment characteristics, and land use using existing empirical models (Peterson and Shea [USGS], unpub. data, 2010). These transition probabilities will then be used to simulate the occupancy of individual segments. Similar to the coarse-resolution approach, we will examine the influence of species traits on the sensitivity of aquatic biota to changes in climate and landscapes. Discharge, temperature, geomorphic stream-segment characteristics, and land use dynamics will each be modeled at fine resolution as described above for each model component.

For all modeling approaches, we will incorporate parametric (statistical) uncertainty by assigning probability distributions to model parameters. Structural uncertainty will be explicitly considered by postulating feasible alternative models, with each model representing a hypothesized relation among inputs, system dynamics, and objectives (Williams

and others, 2002). The final structure of the coarse-resolution models will be in a user-friendly format, such as a Bayes network (Peterson and Evans 2003), to allow biologists to evaluate the relative value of alternative decisions. The fine-resolution models also will be placed in a user-friendly format that will allow biologists to run simulation scenarios based on potential management actions. Sensitivity analysis will then be performed on all models and model inputs to identify and prioritize the key uncertainties.

Phase II—Model Refinement

Phase I will provide comparative models of climate-change effects on fishes and mussels, as estimated using probabilistic projections of climate change in (1) coarse-resolution measures of hydrology, landscape, and geomorphic features to predict relative effects on species in differing portions of the ACF Basin; (2) fine-resolution models of species occupancy dynamics within subbasins of the ACF, as driven by hydrology, temperature, landscape, and geomorphic features measured at finer scales; and (3) coarse-resolution models derived by aggregating results from fine-resolution models. Sensitivity analysis will identify what types of additional data would have the greatest effect in reducing uncertainty in model predictions. Simultaneously, partner research teams will have been developing coarse- and fine-scale models for bird species in the Southeast Region.

Building on these Phase I models, researchers will confer with resource managers to examine the usefulness of coarse- and fine-resolution models for understanding potential climate-change effects with respect to specific conservation goals. In particular, it will be of interest to explore how the appropriate model resolution may depend on characteristics of species and landscapes, and on the factors that most limit priority species. This will provide a basis for developing models that integrate conservation objectives for terrestrial and aquatic priority species. Phase I results will also be used to explore methods for modeling linkages across resolutions so that effects of conservation actions can be analyzed in terms of predicted effects at multiple levels.

We will work with regional fish and wildlife managers to identify priority species and ecoregional areas that appear especially vulnerable to projected climate-change effects and areas where multi-resolution model development could help guide conservation strategies. Understanding and models developed in Phase I will then be used to develop models at appropriate resolutions for those species (terrestrial and aquatic) and to design data-collection strategies that will address the largest sources of uncertainty identified in Phase I. Model components would include probabilistic projections of climate change, spatially explicit hydrology, land-use and land-cover dynamics, and the geomorphic/landform template that constrains and defines habitat characteristics, in a context to predict distributions of species and assemblages under climate and management scenarios.

References

Brim Box, J. and Williams, J.D., 2000, Unionid mollusks of the Apalachicola Basin in Alabama, Florida, and Georgia: Bulletin of the Alabama Museum of Natural History 21.

Bryk, A.S., and Raudenbush, S.W., 2002, Hierarchical linear models—Applications and data analysis methods (2d ed.): Newbury Park, CA, Sage.

Hay, L.E., and Umemoto, Makiko, 2007, Multiple-objective stepwise calibration using Luca: U.S. Geological Survey Open-File Report 2006–1323. 25 p.

Leavesley, G.H., 1983, Precipitation-runoff modeling system: user's manual: U.S. Geological Survey Water-Resources Investigations Report 83–4238, 207 p., available online at *http://pubs.er.usgs.gov/usgspubs/wri/wri834238* [.DJVU format].

Peterson, J.T., and Evans, J.W., 2003, Decision analysis for sport fisheries management: Fisheries, v. 28, no. 1, p. 10–20.

Rieman, B.E., Peterson, J.T., Clayton, J., Howell, P., Thurow, R.F., Thompson, W., and Lee, D.C., 2001, Evaluation of the potential effects of federal land management alternatives on the trends of salmonids and their habitats in the Interior Columbia River Basin: Journal of Forest Ecology and Management, v. 153, p. 43–62.

Ruiz, J., and Peterson, J.T., 2007, An evaluation of the relative influence of spatial, statistical, and biological factors on the accuracy of stream fish species presence models: Transactions of the American Fisheries Society, v. 136, p. 1640–1653.

Viger, R.J., Hay, L.E., Jones, J.W., and Buell, G.R., 2009, Effects of including surface depressions in the application of the Precipitation-Runoff Modeling System in the Upper Flint River Basin, Georgia: U.S. Geological Survey Scientific Investigations Report 2010–5062, 36 p.

Williams, B.K., Nichols, J.D., and Conroy, M.J., 2002, Analysis and management of animal populations: San Diego, CA, Academic Press, 817 p.

Chapter V.   Optimal Conservation Strategies to Cope With Climate Change

By James Grand

Introduction

We propose to develop a framework for using AM and the principles of SHC to address the potential impacts of climate change on terrestrial and aquatic species in the Southeastern United States. AM provides an ideal framework for the establishment and attainment of conservation objectives in the face of tremendous uncertainty, while SHC is specifically designed to address issues associated with establishing and maintaining target populations. Although it can be argued that SHC is only applicable at landscape scales, the iterative nature of both processes is essentially parallel.

AM as defined in the U.S. Department of the Interior Technical Guide (Williams and others, 2007) involves assessment, design, implementation, monitoring, evaluation, and adjustment phases, while SHC requires biological planning, conservation design, implementation, monitoring, and applied research. The assessment and design phases of AM correspond closely with requirements associated with biological planning and conservation design—identification of focal species and their population status, development of population objectives, determination of habitat requirements, inventory of the available resources (habitat), determination of habitat objectives, and configuration of the desired landscape. Additionally, AM provides explicitly for the accommodation of stakeholder input in the establishment of these elements. These steps logically lead to the development of models that predict the results of conservation actions (management or policy) referred to in SHC as decision support tools. An emergent property of using either process in a structured decision-making context is the identification of fundamental objectives that describe the important outcomes of conservation actions, as well as means objectives that describe the actions themselves. This logically leads to the correct identification of the information necessary to understand the state of the system and the models necessary to predict the outcome of system dynamics resulting from changing environments or conservation action.

The development of decision support tools or predictive models in the case of climate change is complicated by structural as well as parametric uncertainty. With adequate forethought, AM can be used to address decisions that are plagued by both sources of uncertainty. By structural uncertainty, we refer to a lack of complete knowledge of the system (the environmental model). Thus, AM may be particularly well suited to decisions related to climate change, since there is great debate regarding nature and magnitude of change. Fish and wildlife agencies are typically faced with making decisions in stochastic but relatively constant environments. Thus, competing environmental models may be used to predict future system states as well as the nature of species' responses. Parametric uncertainty refers to the degree of response elicited by conservation actions. Addressing both sources of uncertainty will require the ability to make relatively precise predictions regarding the environment, the ensuing changes to the resources required by terrestrial and aquatic species, and the effects and responses to conservation actions. Thus, data and models that operate at increasingly finer scales, such as those proposed in the projects outlined here, will be required to learn how the system is evolving over time and whether conservation actions are leading to progress toward the stated objectives.

Finally, AM and SHC require the establishment of implementation plans and monitoring programs that are used to track progress toward objectives. Over time, both types of uncertainty can be reduced through monitoring programs that address the key components and relations that define the system state. The identification of these key components is an emergent property of the process of correctly describing system structure.

Objectives

The primary objective of this project is to develop a framework to implement SHC using AM to determine optimal conservation strategies that incorporate the potential effects of climate change on fish and wildlife populations at an eco-regional scale. For each ecoregion, the following seven tasks will be implemented, based on input from stakeholders in the fish and wildlife conservation community.

Based on input from stakeholders in the fish and wildlife conservation community:

- Identify focal species for planning conservation actions within each ecoregion. Focal species should represent the species most sensitive to resource and process limitations in the Southeast Region (Lambeck, 1997) and should represent a broad array of taxa.

- Assess the state of populations of focal species based on the best available information. This may include survey data (such as BBS, mid-winter waterfowl surveys, North American Amphibian Monitoring Program) or expert opinion.

- Determine population objectives and habitat objectives for focal species that will ensure their persistence.

- Identify and quantify the effects of management and policy alternatives for the conservation of focal species.

- Based on the best available and related projects in this assessment:

- Use habitat relationship models (see Technical Proposals IV and V) for focal species to predict population responses to climate change and conservation actions.

- Determine optimal conservation strategies based on the identified management and policy alternatives that are most likely to sustain populations of focal species.

- Identify key elements for monitoring that will reduce uncertainty regarding the effect of climate change on terrestrial and aquatic populations and their habitats and measure progress toward population and habitat objectives.

Workshops

We will create a structured decision model to identify priorities for the conservation of multiple habitats in the ACF Basin with the goal of linking priorities for both terrestrial and aquatic systems using the frameworks of Strategic Habitat Conservation and Adaptive Management. The first four objectives will be addressed through a series of facilitated workshops for a select group of decision makers and technical experts (stakeholders) from the fish and wildlife conservation community in each Bird Conservation Region of the Southeast

Region. Workshop participants should represent a cross section of State, federal, and non-governmental agencies committed to long-term conservation and participation in the AM process. During the workshops, we will re-evaluate species identified as potentially vulnerable to climate change using a process adapted from Lambeck (1997) to identify species and habitats that are most sensitive to resource (patch size, habitat composition, and connectivity) and process (altered hydrology, altered fire regimes, invasive species, non-native predators) limitations. The species most sensitive to these environmental stressors, especially those expected to be most effected by climate change will be used as focal species for SHC and AM processes. Similar to the suggestions of Lambeck (1997), we will consider species whose regional populations are of conservation concern and those considered especially vulnerable to the effects of climate change (fig. 1).

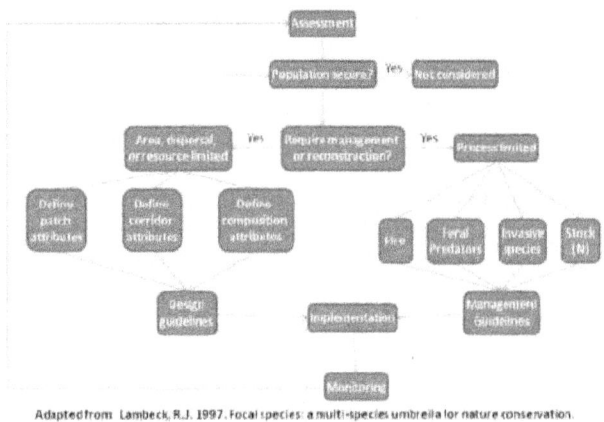

Adapted from Lambeck, R.J. 1997. Focal species: a multi-species umbrella for nature conservation. Conservation Biology 11(4):849-856.

Figure 1.   Conceptual model for the selection of focal species.

The current state of each focal species will be determined through the use of existing data (BBS) or expert opinion solicited during technical meetings following the workshops. We will establish population objectives for focal species beginning with existing conservation plans (North American Waterfowl Management Plan, Shorebird Conservation Plan, Northern Bobwhite Conservation Initiative) and where necessary adjust them to meet long-term objectives for sustainability and utility. Where sufficient data exist and published studies are not available, we will use population viability analyses to establish population objectives related to persistence times.

Workshop participants will be asked to identify ecoregional-scale management and policy alternatives that may affect populations of focal species. Alternatives should include planned actions such as Farm Bill programs, carbon sequestration, conservation-land acquisition, and wetlands protection. We will use input from workshop participants and existing documentation to determine the proposed scope, magnitude, and likelihood for success of the effect of each action with regard to land use and land cover within each ecoregion.

In Phase I of this project, stakeholder input, animal-distribution models, and land-cover-change predictions will be used to develop Bayesian belief and decision networks (Marcot and others, 2006; Nyberg and others, 2006). This will allow us to rapidly prototype model structures, determine the correct parameterization, and assess model sensitivity.

In Phase II we will develop spatially explicit, dynamic models that address the following objectives for each focal species under each of the climate scenarios:

- Determine where suitable sites will occur for the establishment or enhancement of habitat for each focal species over the next 100 years. These models will be based largely on abiotic factors, such as parent material (geology) and land form, but will also include factors influenced by climate such as probable coast lines based on sea-level rise (fig. 2A).

- Determine where constraints exist on our ability to appropriately manage (adapt) for each focal species over the next 100 years. These models will incorporate parameters such as the probable density of urban development, which limits the use of prescribed fire, an essential element in the maintenance of disturbance regimes in some ecosystems (fig. 2B).

- Determine where public lands and land trusts that are likely to be managed for conservation into perpetuity. Where located appropriately, these areas may serve as core areas for the conservation of large patches and corridors of habitat for focal species and co-occurring species of concern. Thus, areas near large tracts of this "conservation estate" are likely targets for conservation action that will have long-term benefits (fig. 2C).

- Determine where potential habitat for focal species exists. These models will be based on habitat relationships for focal species that rely on land cover and landscape characteristics and corresponding predictions under climate-change models (fig 2D). When they are available, we will use habitat-relationship models developed by researchers at the North Carolina CFWRU that incorporate spatial and temporal variation in vital rates (see Conroy and Noon, 1996).

- Determine where potential source populations for focal species exist. Large patches of appropriate habitat with suitable structural characteristics are the most likely locations for source populations that will colonize new or enhanced habitat for focal species and other species with similar habitat requirements (fig 2E).

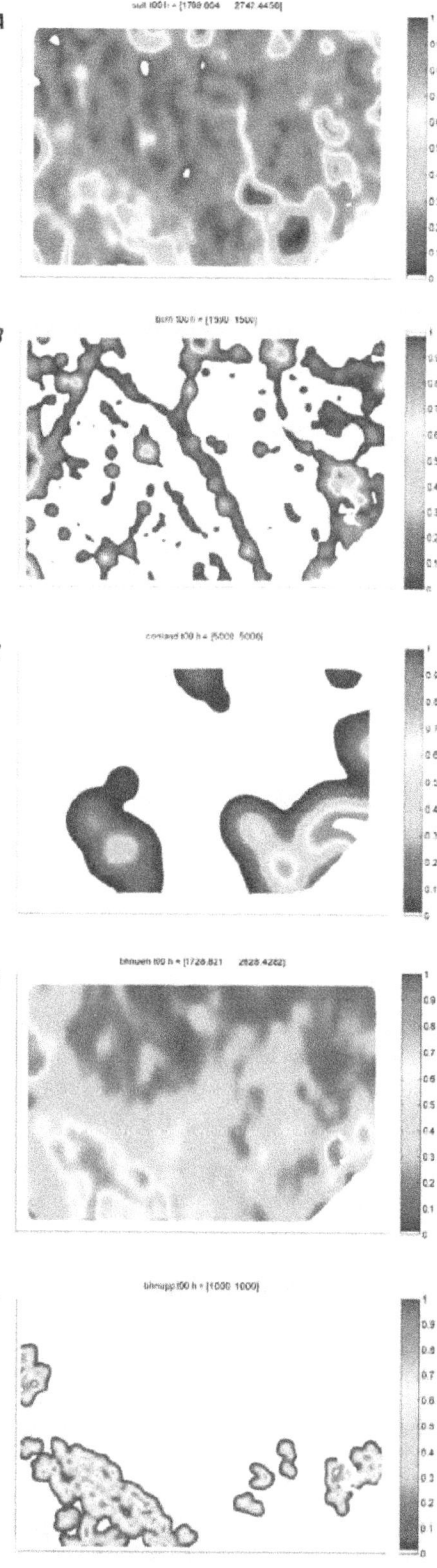

Figure 2. Probability density surfaces used in determining priority for conservation.

When combined, these probabilistic surfaces will identify the most significant locations for conservation actions across multiple species, habitats, and time periods incorporating tradeoffs among multiple focal species and predictions of future conditions, discounted for uncertainties within and among climate projections (fig. 3 and 4). This approach is currently being employed for avian conservation planning in the Gulf and Atlantic coastal plains based on static landscapes and will be extended to include competing models for animal response and conservation priority.

These models will be used to examine the probable effectiveness of alternative potential conservation policies for adaptation to climate change. By incorporating uncertainty in the form of subscription and compliance to policies identified by stakeholders, the effectiveness of various policies can be compared and tradeoffs evaluated by estimating contributions to conservation measured by changes in the volume under the priority surface. We will include stochastic dynamic processes by the iterative simulation of policies and updating of the priority surface.

References

Conroy, M.J., and Noon, B.R., 1996, Mapping of species richness for conservation of biological diversity—Conceptual and methodological issues: Ecological Applications, v. 6, p. 763–773.

Lambeck, R.J. 1997. Focal species—A multi-species umbrella for nature conservation: Conservation Biology, v. 11, no. 4, p. 849–856.

Marcot, B.G., Steventon, J.D., Sutherland, G.D., and McCann, R.K., 2006, Guidelines for developing and updating Bayesian belief networks applied to ecological modeling and conservation: Canadian Journal of Forest Research, v. 36, p. 3063–3074.

Nyberg, J.B., Marcot, B.G., and Sulyma, R., 2006, Using Bayesian belief networks in adaptive management: Canadian Journal of Forest Research, v. 36, p. 3104–3116.

Williams, B.K., Szaro, R.C., and Shapiro, C.D., 2007, Adaptive management—The U.S. Department of the Interior Technical Guide: Adaptive Management Working Group, U.S. Department of the Interior, Washington, DC.

U.S. Fish and Wildlife Service, 2008, Strategic habitat conservation handbook—A guide to implementing the technical elements of strategic habitat conservation (version 1.0): Washington, DC, National Technical Assistance Team, U.S. Fish and Wildlife Service.

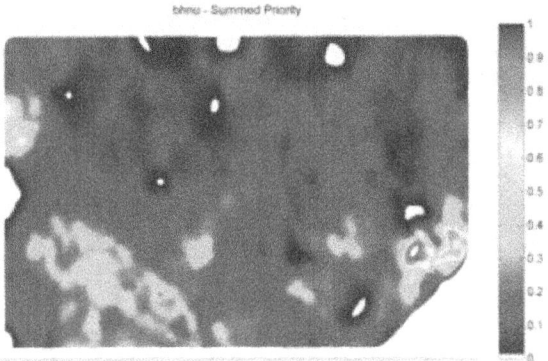

Figure 3. Spatially explicit conservation priority based on conditional probabilities of resource distributions.

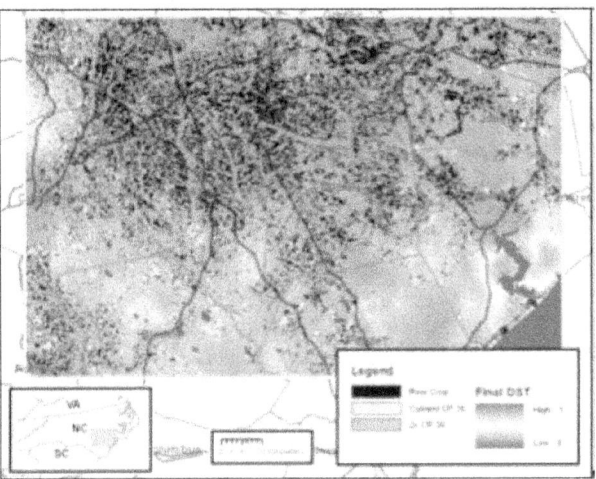

Figure 4. Application of a spatially explicit conservation policy to selected land cover types based on conservation priority. Black areas indicate current row crop, yellow areas simulate the allocation of conservation policy to crop lands within highest priority areas. Orange patches indicate a larger application of the same policy.

Chapter VI.   Development and Dissemination of High-Resolution National Climate Change Dataset

Jaime Collazo, Lauren Hay, Katharine Hayhoe, Nathaniel Booth, and Adam Terando

Introduction

We propose to create a comprehensive Web-based database of high-resolution climate-change projections that can be used to assess the impacts of climate change on ecosystems throughout the continental United States. The dataset will be generated by applying advanced statistical downscaling methods to a comprehensive selection of global model simulations from the IPCC AR4 database. This project will develop high-resolution climate-modeling information and derivative products necessary to project ecological and population responses to climate change at regional levels. In addition, we will also communicate with and gather input from the climate-change research community concerning climate downscaling-data needs, best practices, and methodological issues that foster greater understanding of climate-change projections.

The proposed work will serve three purposes: (1) allow for consistent impact assessments at the scale of the most critical ecosystem processes through downscaling projections of daily temperature, precipitation, and other impact-relevant variables across the continental United States; (2) enable scientists and managers to easily access, manipulate and download data relevant to modeling climate-change impacts on ecosystems through a common Web-based data portal; and (3) explore ways to potentially reduce redundant efforts to obtain and produce downscaled climate data by soliciting feedback from the climate-change research community in a workshop setting.

The ultimate goal of this work is to enable impact assessments to be based on the same common dataset, allowing consistent results to be compared across regions and ecosystems. By standardizing approaches to data processing and provision, we will minimize redundancy of data gathering by modelers, systematize and improve data quality assurance procedures specific to the simulation models, and reduce the likelihood of misinterpretation or misuse of data content.

We will develop and test this service using national-scale climate projections derived from a pilot study already funded by the USGS NCCWSC as part of the SERAP. The final product will be made available to all interested in assessing the effects of climate change on their particular field, with the goal of ensuring consistent and correctly applied climate projections and methodologies for local, regional, and continental scale studies.

Background

Model analyses and inter-comparisons have shown that the latest generation of coupled AOGCMs provide a reasonable representation of observed climate change at the global scale over the last century (Parry et al., 2007). However, global-scale changes in the climate system interact with distinctive geographic characteristics of individual areas around the world to produce unique regional signals. For that reason, high-resolution regional projections of climate change are required to accurately evaluate how climate change is likely to affect a given system. The utility of regional climate projections as a means to assess impacts on different ecosystems, flora, and fauna has been demonstrated by a number of recent publications (e.g., Fogarty et al. 2008; Hayhoe et al., 2007; Iverson et al., 2008; Loarie et al., 2008; Rodenhouse et al., 2008).

Application of state-of-the-art high-resolution climate projections to impact studies, particularly in the area of ecology, has been hindered in the past by the lack of a standard methodology for generating these projections. This deficiency has led to many regional impact studies based on climate projections from outdated global models and scenarios, and/or using elementary downscaling techniques such as bias removal or a "delta" approaches that correct only for model biases in the monthly mean. This lack of a standardized source for climate projections has rendered the quality of many otherwise excellent studies questionable, as well as complicating efforts to compare the results of individual studies across the same region.

To address these issues, we propose a two-part process for providing high-resolution climate data for the impact modeling community. First, we propose to establish a database of up-to-date downscaled climate projections for the entire United States for a range of plausible future emission scenarios. Second, we will make these data available online as a comprehensive, Web-based source where users can freely access these projections via an interactive, easily manageable interface and in formats that are familiar to ecosystem and impact modelers.

The proposed Web-based Geo Data Portal (GDP) will enable every impact study requiring basic climate inputs to be based on the same common dataset, allowing consistent results to be compared across regions and ecosystems. By standardizing approaches to data processing and provision, the portal will minimize the redundancy and effort of data gathering by modelers, systematize and improve data-quality-assurance procedures specific to the climate models, and reduce the likelihood of misinterpretation or misuse of data content.

Methods

Downscaled Climate Projections

The national climate-change database will be generated using advanced statistical downscaling techniques that take advantage of the physical relations between the climate simulated by large-scale AOGCMs and the observed climate in the region of interest. Advantages to statistical downscaling include that the methods are cost and time efficient, they are easily transferable to other regions, and they have the ability to directly incorporate observations into the downscaling method. The primary disadvantage of statistical downscaling is the assumption of stationarity in the predictor-predictand relation, which assumes little to no change in the climate system feedback mechanisms through time (Wilby, 1998). However, the precipitation method we use here has been tested directly against future simulations by a dynamic regional climate model, indicating the assumption of stationarity holds in future decades past the 99th quantile of the distribution (Vrac et al., 2007a).

For temperature we employ an asynchronous quantile regression method that can determine relations between two quantities not measured simultaneously, such as an observed and a model-simulated time series. The method assumes that although the two time series are independent they describe the same variable, at approximately the same location, and therefore must have similar PDFs. We then regress the two independent time-varying variables $X(t)$ and $Y(t)$ using only their statistical distributions $F(x)$ and $G(y)$. The method determines the function $Y=u(X)$ by matching the quantiles of x and y of the distributions of X and Y for each probability level (O'Brien et al., 2001). Using daily model-simulated maximum and minimum air temperature from the AOGCM as the predictor, and daily observed maximum and minimum temperatures as the predictand, the resulting regression model can then force the PDFs of the simulated temperature fields to match those of the observed data for the training period (fig. 1A). These relations are then tested against observations for a historical evaluation period (fig. 1B).

For precipitation, methods using upper air fields, such as temperature, humidity, and geopotential height as predictors of surface precipitation, tend to exhibit a significantly larger degree of skill than methods using surface precipitation as a predictor. For that reason, to downscale daily precipitation we

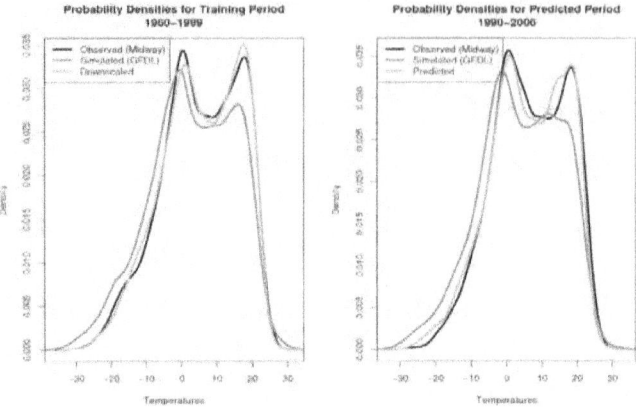

Figure 1. Probability densities for the training period (1969–1989) (left) and evaluation period (1990–2006) (right). The black line is observed minimum temperature from Midway Airport in Chicago, the red line is the minimum temperature simulated by the global model GFDL-CM2.1 for the grid cell containing Midway Airport, and the green line is the fit regressed by the downscaling model.

employ a nonhomogeneous stochastic categorization and transition approach that provides accurate and rapid simulations of local-scale precipitation based on statistically defined weather states derived from 850mb geopotential height, humidity, and dew point temperature (Vrac et al., 2007b). The accuracy of the method is enhanced by use of a hierarchical ascending clustering method to identify surface precipitation patterns that characterize conditional distributions and intensity of rainfall across a larger geographical area. Evaluation of this method using independent observations indicates it is accurate up to individual events of 4 centimeters or greater. Comparison to regional model simulations indicates future stationarity of this method at quantiles up to the 99th percentile of the distribution (Vrac et al., 2007a).

Geo Data Portal

The GDP (fig. 2) is a Web-delivered computer application for identification, selection, extraction, processing, quality control, and formatting of spatio-temporal data for ecosystem modeling applications. The purpose is to bring modelers (researchers who require input datasets for their models) and data providers (researchers who have processed, synthesized, or otherwise produced information that can be used by the modelers) together in a common framework. While the initial intent of the GDP is to disseminate the High-Resolution National Climate Change Dataset, the platform and framework of the Portal could support other data dissemination needs.

It is crucial to the intended purpose of the GDP that the proposed interface be straightforward, easy to use, and provides the data, services and formats required by the primary users. To this end, we propose, first, to conduct an internal review of the usability of existing data portals that provide geodata to users. In addition to portals developed

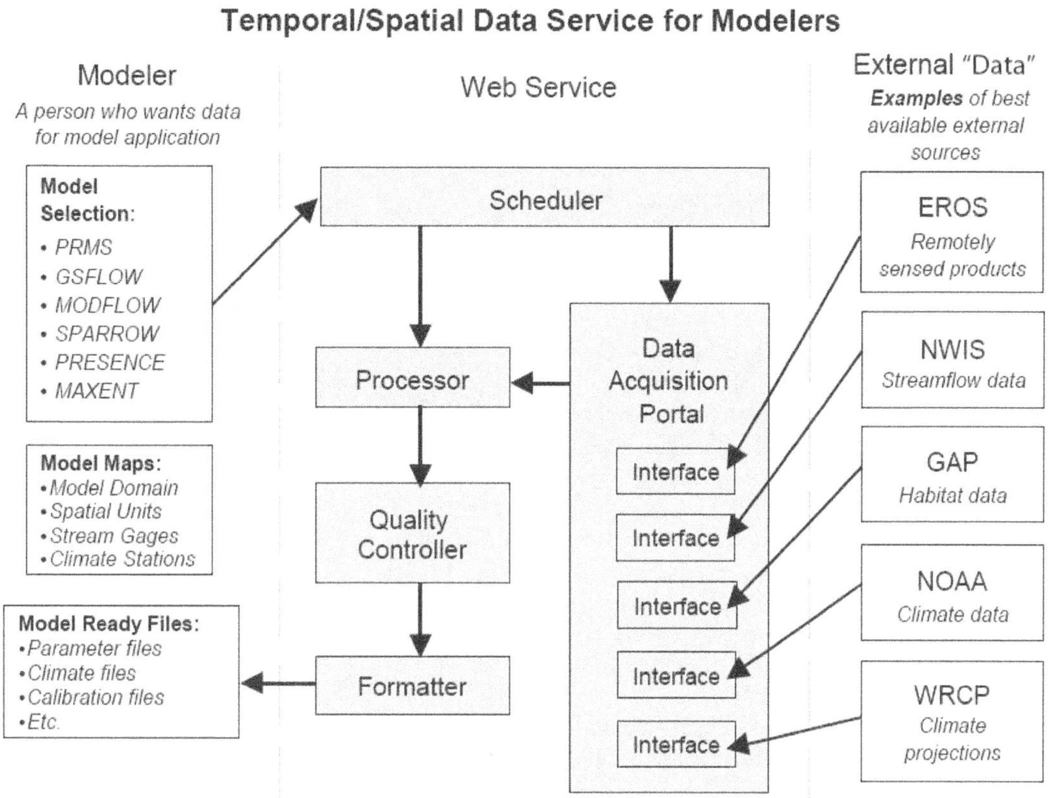

Temporal/Spatial Data Service for Modelers

Modeler	Web Service	External "Data"
A person who wants data for model application		*Examples of best available external sources*

Model Selection:
- *PRMS*
- *GSFLOW*
- *MODFLOW*
- *SPARROW*
- *PRESENCE*
- *MAXENT*

Model Maps:
- *Model Domain*
- *Spatial Units*
- *Stream Gages*
- *Climate Stations*

Model Ready Files:
- *Parameter files*
- *Climate files*
- *Calibration files*
- *Etc.*

Scheduler

Processor

Quality Controller

Formatter

Data Acquisition Portal

Interface
Interface
Interface
Interface
Interface

EROS
Remotely sensed products

NWIS
Streamflow data

GAP
Habitat data

NOAA
Climate data

WRCP
Climate projections

Figure 2.   Schematic of Geo Data Portal server inputs, internal data acquisition and provision, and outputs.

by the principal investigators, other sites to be considered in the survey include but are not limited to the World Climate Research Program CMIP3 multi-model database, the National Climatic Data Center, Climate Wizard, the Earth System Grid, the U.S. Department of Energy Green Data Oasis, and the Columbia University Center for International Earth Science Information Network. This survey is intended to provide initial guidance in design of the GDP interface.

The first dataset we propose to host at the GDP is a nationally downscaled set of future daily temperature and precipitation projections, as described previously. The data will exist as sets of metadata, gridded data, time-series data, etc., that could be stored in remote geo-databases, ftp sites, or Web services. Making this data available through the GDP will require custom programs, as represented by the Interface boxes in the figure 2. Each Interface will access data from its respective Data Provider so more can be added to the GDP independently of any other Data Providers or Modelers. This will allow us to develop and test the protocols required for the Interface programs without having to identify future Data Providers.

Once one or more Data Providers are interfaced to the GDP, Modelers can start to access this data. A Modeler begins his or her session by logging into the GDP. A specific model, relevant maps (defining spatial extent), as well as other information (e.g. time period, resolution, units, etc.) are specified through the GDP interface. The Scheduler receives

this request and begins calling the appropriate Interfaces to retrieve the requested data from the Data Providers. After the data is acquired, it is passed on to the Processor. Depending on the type of data, the Processor could execute geo-processing programs (e.g. zonal statistics related to the Modeler's maps), temporal aggregation or disaggregation, unit conversion, etc. For the Nationally Downscaled Climate Change Dataset, the first programs in the Processor library will clip the data to the required spatial domain and provide areal-weighted averages related to the Modeler's spatial units. As more and more Data Providers and Modelers are added to the GDP, the functional capabilities of the Processor will be expanded.

Before the requested data is passed back to the Modeler, it is first passed through the Quality Controller. The initial version of the Quality Controller will identify outlying data points. In time, more sophisticated methods could be developed and incorporated. Finally, the data passes to the Formatter. The Formatter contains specific programs that will write input files in the correct format for the respective models.

Once an interface for the GDP has been developed, we will conduct a second survey and workshop using a limited group of users (drawing from the more than 400 users of the Northeast Climate Impacts Assessment data site). The purpose will be to evaluate the proposed design of the GDP site, elucidating user critiques and suggestions that can be incorporated into the final design.

Workshops

An important objective of this work is to provide information to end users of downscaled climate data in the most efficient and useful manner possible. As part of our plan to achieve this goal, we will hold a series of facilitated workshops to solicit input and disseminate information from researchers involved with SERAP. The first workshop will involve climate-change researchers. Participants will describe how downscaling approaches are used in their work and provide feedback on useful climatic variables relevant to ecosystem modeling efforts. In addition, the workshop will be an opportunity for participants to learn about different downscaling methods, global-climate models, best practices for use of climate data (both observations and model output), and the structure of the proposed national downscaled climate dataset.

The second workshop would take the form of a half-day short course on global climate models, downscaling techniques, and the planned GDP. Finally, as described in the Geo Portal Section, we will hold a final workshop with potential data users to evaluate the proposed design of the GDP. These workshops will improve our final deliverables but also improve knowledge within the USGS and DOI community about climate-change science and climate-change scenarios.

Summary

The primary product from this work is an interactive GDP (with appropriate user instructions) that allows researchers to access a consistent, standardized set of high-resolution daily climate projections encompassing the widest feasible range of emission scenarios. This online data portal will also be designed to allow for the incorporation of additional geo datasets as funding and information becomes available.

There are five main venues for information transfer throughout this project: workshops, scientific literature, popular literature, teaching, and the Web-based interactive tool. In its own right, the GDP will provide constant access to modeled scenarios for the general public and importantly, for natural-resource managers and ecosystem modelers. The workshops will provide direct opportunities for information and technology transfer to DOI stakeholders.

References

Fogarty, M., Incze, L., Hayhoe, K., Mountain, D., and Manning, J., 2008, Potential climate change impacts on Atlantic cod (Gadusmorhua) off the northeastern USA: Mitigation and Adaptation Strategies for Global Change, v. 13, 5–6, p. 453–466.

Hayhoe, K., Wake, C., Huntington, T., Luo, L., Schwartz, M., Sheffield, J., Wood, E., Anderson, B., Bradbury, J., DeGaetano, A., Troy, T., and Wolfe, D., 2007, Past and future changes in climate and hydrological indicators in the U.S. Northeast: Climate Dynamics, 28, p. 381–407, DOI 10.1007/s00382-006-0187-8.

Iverson, L. R., Prasad, A.M., Matthews, S. N., and Peters, M., 2008, Estimating potential habitat for 134 eastern U.S. tree species under six climate scenarios: Forest Ecology and Management 254(3), p. 390–406.

Loarie, S., Carter, B., Hayhoe, K., Moe, R., Knight, C., and Ackerly, D., 2008, Climate change and the fate of California's endemic flora: PLoS ONE 3, 6, e2502. doi:10.1371/journal.pone.0002502.

O'Brien, T.P., Sornette, D., and McPherron, R.L., 2001, Statistical asynchronous regression—Determining the relationship between two quantities that are not measure simultaneously: Journal of Geophysical Research, v. 106, no. A7, p. 13,247–13,259.

Parry, M.L., Canziani, O.F., Palutikof, J.P., van der Linden, P.J., and Hanson, C.E., eds., 2007, Climate change 2007—Impacts, adaptation and vulnerability: Contributions of Working Group II to the Fourth Assessment Report of the Intergovernmental Panel on Climate Change, Cambridge University Press, Cambridge, UK.

Rodenhouse, N., Matthews, S., McFarland, K., Lambert, J., Iverson, L., Prasad, A., Sillet, T., and Holmes, R., 2008, Potential effects of climate change on birds of the Northeast—Mitigation and adaptation strategies for global change: DOI 10.1007/s11027-007-9126-1.

U.S. Global Change Research Program, 2009: Global climate change impacts in the United States: NOAA/USGCRP Report, available online at *http://www.globalchange.gov/usimpacts.*

Vrac, M., Stein, M., Hayhoe, K., and Liang, X.Z., 2007a, A general method for validating statistical downscaling methods under future climate change: Geophysical Research Letters, 34, L18701.

Vrac, M., Stein, M., and Hayhoe, K., 2007b: Statistical downscaling of precipitation through a nonhomogeneous stochastic weather typing approach: Climate Research, v. 34, p. 169–184.

Wilby, R.L., Wigley, T.M.L., Conway, D., Jones, P.D., Hewitson, B.C., Main, J., and Wilks, D.S., 1998a, Statistical downscaling of general circulation model output—A comparison of methods: Water Resources Research, v. 34, p. 2995–3008.

Manuscript approved for publication, August 23, 2010

Edited by John M. Watson

Layout by Caryl J. Wipperfurth

For more information concerning the research in this report, contact

Melinda S. Dalton
USGS Georgia Water Science Center
3039 Amwiler Road
Atlanta, Georgia 30360

telephone: 770-903-9100
http://ga.water.usgs.gov

Dalton, M.S., and Jones, S.A., comps.—Southeast Regional Assessment Project for the National Climate Change and Wildlife Science Center, USGS—Open-File Report 2010–1213

≋USGS